OSTIA SPEAKS

OSTIA SPEAKS

Inscriptions, buildings and spaces in Rome's main port

L. Bouke van der Meer

PEETERS
LEUVEN – PARIS – WALPOLE, MA

Cover illustration: marble altar for the Lares of the Neighbourhood (photo author).

Cover folder: map of Ostia (courtesy Archivio Fotografico della Soprintendenza Speciale per i Beni Archeologici di Roma e Ostia; numbers added by J. Porck).

© 2012 Peeters, Bondgenotenlaan 153, 3000 Leuven

All rights reserved, including the right to translate or reproduce this book or parts in any form

ISBN 978-90-429-2700-1
D/2012/0602/119

CONTENTS

PREFACE — VIII

INTRODUCTION — 1

CHAPTER 1. BACKGROUNDS — 4

1. A Short History of Ostia — 4
   1.1. The earliest period — 4
   1.2. Growth and boom — 5
   1.3. Decline and a short revival — 8
2. The Political Organisation of Ostia — 9

CHAPTER 2. IN SITU INSCRIPTIONS — 11

1 The Monument for the Well-Being of Caesar Augustus — 11
2 The Inscriptions of Porta Romana — 14
3 The Baths of the Chariot Drivers (II, ii, 3) — 15
4 The Bar of Fortunatus (II, vi, 1) — 19
5 The Barracks of the Firemen (II, v, 1) — 20
6 The Theatre (II, vii, 2) — 27
7 The Square of the Guilds (II, vii, 4) — 31
   7.1. The statue bases in the garden of the Square of the Guilds — 37
8 The Shrine of the Altar of the Twins (II, vii, 3) — 42
9 The Four Small Temples (II, viii, 2) — 45
10 The Sanctuary of Jupiter (II, viii, 4) — 46
11 The Pertinax Inscription and the Guild Temple of the Builders (V, ii, 1) — 47
12 The Boundary Stones of the Public Domain (V, ix, 2) — 48
13 The Small Base for Neptune, Castor and Pollux (I, xii, 3) — 50
14 The Sanctuary of the Lares Vicinales (I, ii, 1) — 51
15 The Apartment building of Jupiter and Ganymedes (I, iv, 2) — 53

CONTENTS

16	THE FORUM	53
17	THE GUILD-HOUSE OF THE BUILDERS (I, xii, 1)	56
18	THE FORUM BATHS (I, xii, 6)	558
19	THE STOREHOUSE OF EPAGATHUS AND EPAPHRODITUS (I, viii, 3)	62
20	THE BATHS VAN BUTICOSUS (I, xiv, 8)	62
21	THE SACRED AREA OF THE HERCULES TEMPLE (I, xv, 5)	63
22	THE MITHRAEUM UNDER THE BATHS OF MITHRAS (I, xvii, 2)	68
23	THE HALL OF THE GRAIN MEASURERS (I, xix, 3)	70
24	THE BATHS OF THE SEVEN WISE MEN (III, x, 2)	72
25	THE BATHS OF TRINACRIA (III, xvi, 7)	74
26	THE SERAPEUM (III, xvii, 4)	76
27	THE HOUSE OF ANNIUS (III, xiv, 4)	78
28	THE HOUSE OF THE THUNDERBOLT (III, vii, 3)	79
29	THE MAUSOLEUM OF C. CARTILIUS POPLICOLA (IV, ix, 2)	80
30	THE SANCTUARY OF BONA DEA (IV, viii, 3)	82
31	THE BAR OF ALEXANDER AND HELIX (IV, vii, 4)	84
32	THE TEMPLE OF THE SHIPBUILDERS (III, ii, 2)	87
33	THE so-called CHRISTIAN BASILICA (III, i, 4)	88
34	THE SHOPS OF THE FISHMONGERS AND THE SO-CALLED MEAT MARKET (IV, v, 1-2)	90
35	THE HOUSE OF THE DESCENDING ZEUS (IV, iv, 3)	92
36	THE HOUSE OF THE FISHES (IV, iii, 3)	94
37	THE CAMPUS OF MAGNA MATER (IV, i)	98
38	THE PAVEMENT OF THE BOUNDARY STONES (V, i)	102
39	THE SHOP OF THE JEALOUS MAN (V, v, 2)	104
40	THE MITHRAEUM OF FELICISSIMUS (V, ix, 1)	104
41	THE GRANARY OF HORTENSIUS (V, xii, 1)	107
42	THE CEMETERY OF VIA OSTIENSIS	109
	42.1. The Tomb of Hermogenes	109
	42.2. A tomb-door with inscription	112
	42.3. A sarcophagus	114

CONTENTS

| APPENDIX 1 | 115 |

EPIGRAPHIC ABBREVIATIONS

| APPENDIX 2 | 117 |

THE REIGNS OF ROMAN EMPERORS

| APPENDIX 3 | 119 |

THE INSCRIPTION IN HONOUR OF P. LUCILIUS GAMALA 'SENIOR'

| APPENDIX 4 | 121 |

THE INSCRIPTION IN HONOUR OF P. LUCILIUS GAMALA 'JUNIOR'

| BIBLIOGRAPHY | 123 |

| INDEX | 126 |

Hic ego qui sine voce loquor de marmore caeso…
Here I am who speaks without voice from cut marble…
(*CIL* XIV 480)

PREFACE

Ancient Ostia is one of the largest and most interesting excavation sites in Italy. While the small city of Pompeii existed from the 6th century BC until the eruption of the Vesuvius in AD 79, Ostia's history can be traced from prehistory until the 9th century AD. *Roman Ostia*, a monumental monograph dealing with most aspects of the city was published by Russell Meiggs in 1960, followed in 1973 by a second revised and extended edition. Some of his conclusions, however, are no longer tenable in light of archaeological and epigraphic research of the last decades. The best archaeological guide is Carlo Pavolini's *Ostia*, published in 1983, followed in 2006 by a new, completely revised edition, both published in Italian. The best book on daily life was published by the same author in 1986 and is entitled *La vita quotidiana a Ostia* (see bibliography).

Ostia's buildings, mosaics and paintings are eye-catching. Inscriptions draw our attention too (see the quotation above) but often their contents are not or less easily understood. In this booklet I attempt to translate and explain them.

Most in situ Latin and Greek inscriptions, related to a building or space, are presented here and, for the first time, provided with an English translation, followed by a short contextual comment. This book is intended not only for scholars, teachers and students, but also for historians, classicists, philologists, linguists, epigraphists, archaeologists and art historians. Comments are based on a critical evaluation of recent archaeological, historical and epigraphic publications, as well as on own research.

The inscriptions cast light upon ideological, religious, funerary and everyday customs and mentalities of people from all ranks of Ostian society - slaves (*servi* and *servae*), house and emperor's slaves (*vernae*), freedmen and -women (*liberti* and *libertae*) and free people (*ingenui* and *ingenuae*) - between ca 100 BC and the beginning of the 5th century AD. Probably only a minority of the population could read and write Latin and/or Greek. On the other hand, some slaves, often of non-Roman origin, could read and write as is evident from votive and funerary inscriptions.

Ostian inscriptions inform us about Roman state and local politics, planning, propaganda, benefaction, memorizing, neighbourliness, pagan, emperor and Christian cults, infrastructure, firemen, so-called guilds (which were usually clubs or societies of entrepreneurs), professions, commerce, bathing, sports, consumption, special events, lust, love and emotions.

All inscriptions were studied and photographed on the spot by Natalie L.C. Stevens and the author in 2003 and 2007 thanks to financial support provided by the Faculty of Archaeology at Leiden University, for which I am grateful. Natalie wrote the Dutch reader of many in situ inscriptions. It was used by students during excursions to and urban fieldwork in Ostia. The present text is a revised, extended and updated edition. A last on-site check took place in 2011.

Harry W. Pleket read my manuscript. His criticism was extremely useful to me.

Useful suggestions were offered by Maria Teresa Lazzarini, Carlo Pavolini, Vania di Stefano, Zahra Newby, Matthew D. Panciera, Hans van Rossum, Jan Theo Bakker, Rolf Tybout, Jos van der Vin (†), Patrick Gouw and Maarten van Deventer. My warm thanks go to Natalie Stevens, to the Faculty Board and to Joanne Porck who added site numbers to a recent plan of Ostia (see cover folder). I am indebted to Lily and Jelle van der Meer for doing the layout, to Peeters Publishers, and to Alistair Bright for correcting my English. Of course, all remaining errors are my own responsibility. Last but not least I am grateful to the *Soprintendenza Speciale per i Beni Archeologici di Roma e Ostia*, particularly to Angelo Pellegrino, Elvira Angeloni, the *Soprintendente* Anna Maria Moretti and the unforgettable, former *Soprintendente* Anna Gallina Zevi. Oxford University Press, in the person of Shelag Phillips, gave me permission to reproduce Ostia's map (see pp. X-XI), published as a large folder in Meiggs' *Roman Ostia* (London 1973[2]).

L. Bouke van der Meer

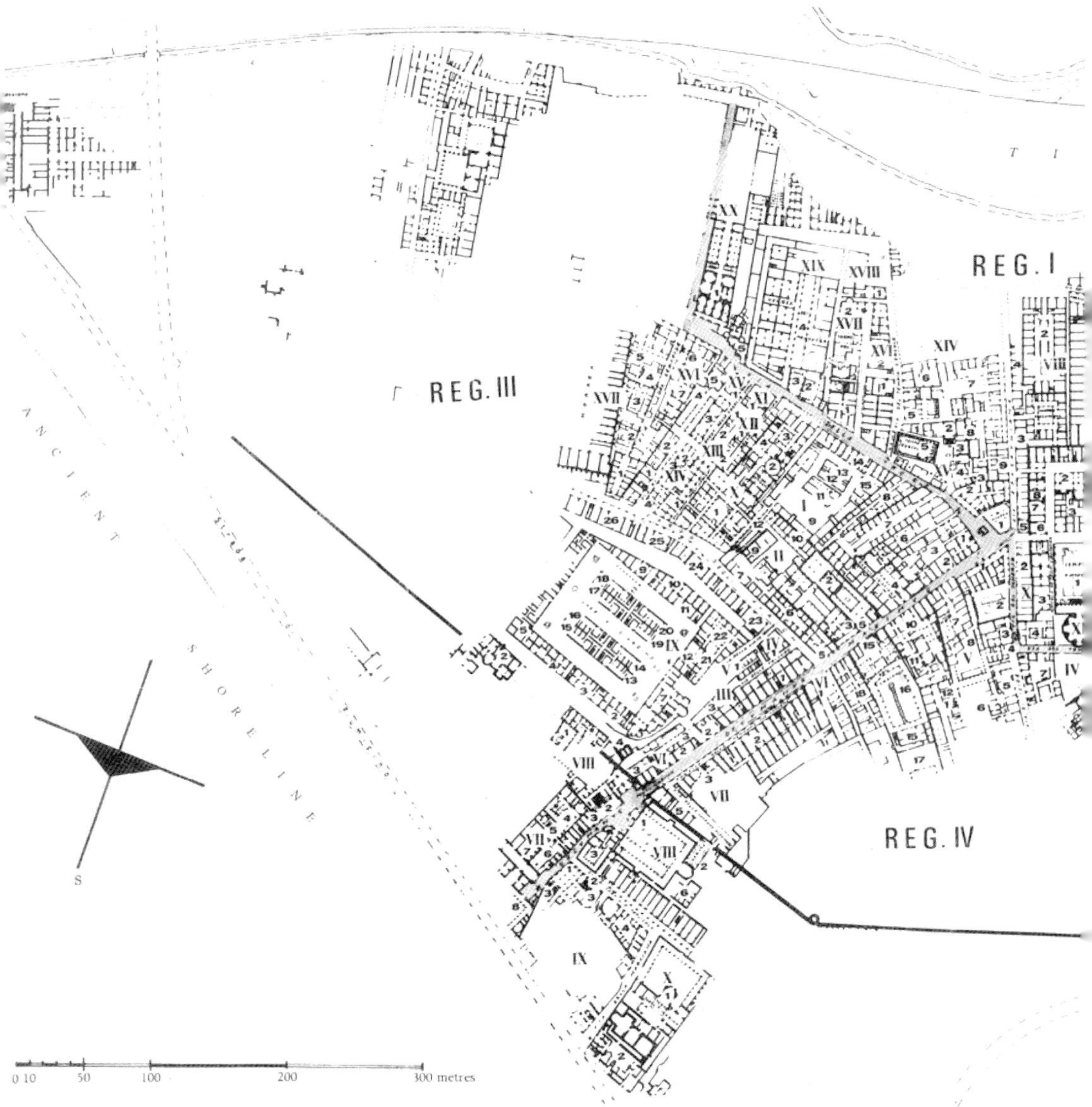
REG. I
REG. III
REG. IV
ANCIENT SHORELINE
S
0 10 50 100 200 300 metres

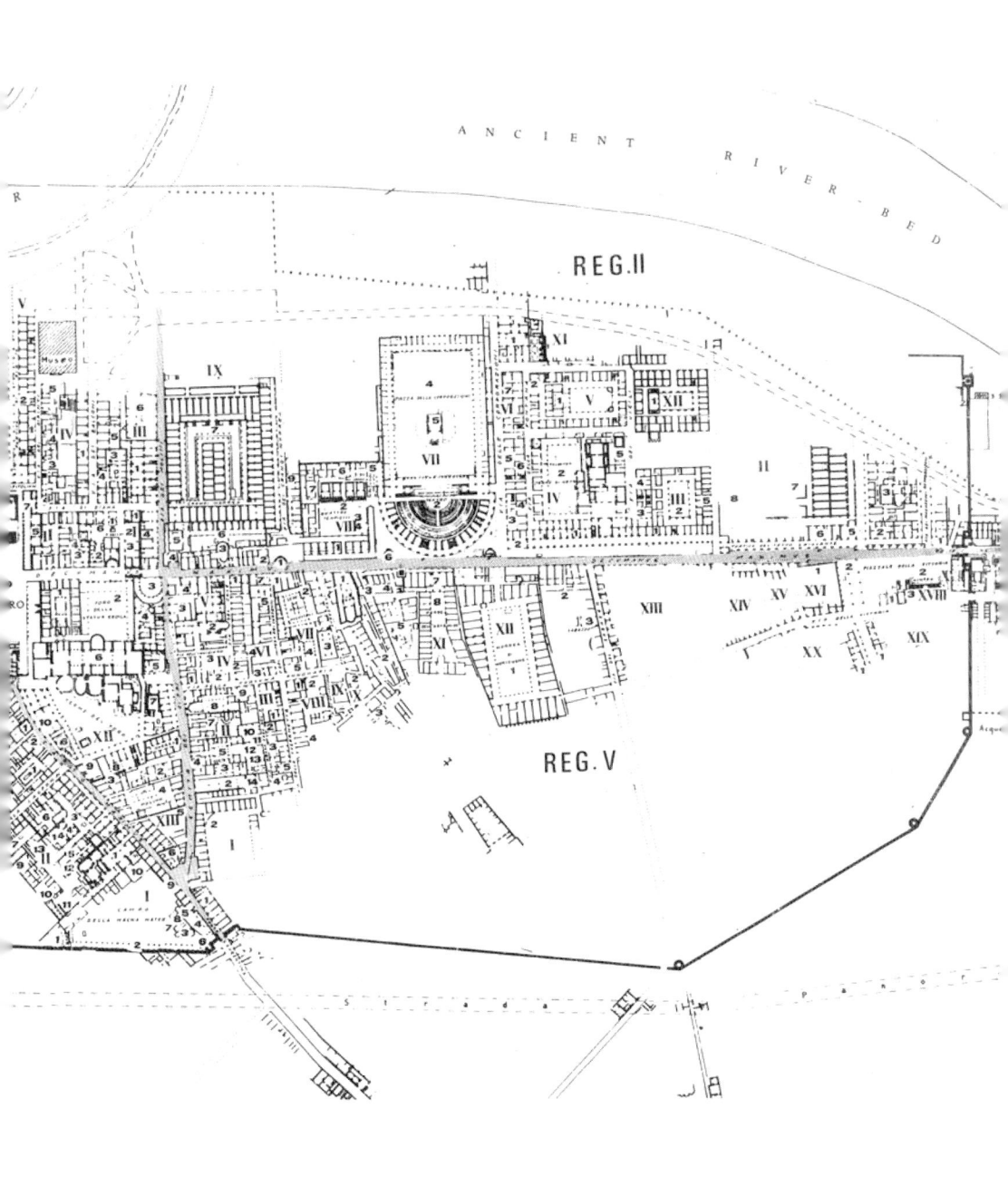

Map of Ostia (from R. Meiggs 1973; courtesy of Oxford University Press).

Columns in front of the Temple of the Shipbuilders (drawing Natalie L.C. Stevens).

INTRODUCTION

The history of Rome's harbour city Ostia covers more than one thousand years, from ca 400 BC until ca 600 AD. The last few inhabitants abandoned the site in the 9th century when it was attacked by the Saracenes.

Most buildings that have been partly preserved date to the 2nd century AD. They often underwent alteration, repair, partial demolition or addition in later centuries. More than fifty ancient authors make mention of Ostia but generally in cursory fashion. As a result, Ostia's history and building history are mainly reconstructed on the basis of archaeological research and inscriptions, especially the brick stamps carrying the names of consuls. Inscriptions are present in or on buildings, in public and sacred spaces, and in or on tombs. Many inscribed artefacts recovered during early excavations have been transferred to museums in Rome and elsewhere, whereas those recovered during 20th century excavations are housed in the local Lapidarium and Museum and its stores at the excavation site. The total number of inscriptions from Ostia and Portus (the harbours of Claudius and Trajan near Ostia) and their cemeteries now numbers around 6500. More than 1500 are funerary in character.

This monograph focuses on the most important in situ inscriptions, in or on buildings (pediments, architraves, mosaics, paintings) and on altars, statue bases and funerary monuments and objects. It intends to clarify the relation between monuments, spaces and people. Some inscribed objects were already transferred to or replaced and reused within Ostia in antiquity. Gravestones from cemeteries outside the city were reused in ground floors of buildings and as toilet seats from the middle of the 3rd century AD onwards. Sometimes statue bases were turned over or placed upside down. A new inscription was then incised on the back. In the Middle Ages, many marble objects were transferred to local lime-kilns. Some never reached the kilns but did not stay in their original location all the same.

The selected Latin and Greek inscriptions are translated and commented on. There are no notes. Whenever scholars are mentioned, their publications can be found in the bibliography.

As for buildings and spaces with inscriptions, only those that are open to the public are dealt with (except for no 15). If there are many statue bases with inscriptions in one space, for example in the Barracks of the Firemen (Caserma dei Vigili) and on the Square of the Guilds (Piazzale delle Corporazioni), a selection has been made. The inscriptions in these locations that are not commented upon are listed with a reference to *Corpus Inscriptionum Latinarum* (*CIL*), volume XIV and its supplement (S), to *L'Année Épigraphique* (*AE*) and to *Supplementum Epigraphicum Graecum* (*SEG*). Every inscription is rendered in its original form, in capital characters. Stops between words (dots, triangular and other signs) have been omitted. The character V with the value of U (pronounce: u:/, as in the word *you*) is rendered as U. The C in the common first name Caius has the value of G. Abbreviated words and names have been completed between brackets, e.g. ANN(onae). Missing characters are rendered in capitals placed between square brackets, e.g. [SE]PTIMIUS. Characters between {...} represent an error by the letter-cutter and should be disregarded. The / symbol indicates a division between lines.

The translations in Chapter 2 are sometimes rather literal to enable the reader to understand the syntax of Latin texts. In complex texts, the subject (subj.) and object (obj.) in a phrase are indicated. The locations with inscriptions are numbered on the map (see cover folder). The generally modern names of a location or building are rendered in English and Italian, followed by for example, IV, iv, 4, which stands for *Regio* IV, *insula* iv (block iv), entrance number 4 (see map pp. X-XI). The Latin word *insula* means apartment building or block of buildings but in this case stands for a part of a city quarter, usually a building, conglomeration of buildings and/or an open space, sometimes bordered by one or more streets. The division into five regions is modern. Ancient Ostia was also divided into five regions (*CIL* XIV 352) but their dimensions and precise location are unknown.

Approximate dates are rendered in a short way. For example, around AD 400 means the period at the end of the 4th century and the beginning of the 5th century.

The appendices contain a list of epigraphic abbreviations and the regnal years of Roman emperors.

Summary of symbols

[---] number of missing characters is unknown
[...] number of dots indicates the number of missing characters
[[ ]] gap in the text; characters are erased because of a *damnatio memoriae*

[xx] missing characters, e.g. [SE]PTIMIUS
{...} characters to be eliminated
(...) completion of an abbreviation
/ start of a new line

Abbreviations of frequently occurring references
(see also Bibliography)

AE *L'Année Épigraphique* (supplement of *Revue Archéologique*), Paris 1888 -.
CIL *Corpus Inscriptionum Latinarum*, Berolini (Berlin) 1863 -.
SEG *Supplementum Epigraphicum Graecum*, Leiden 1923 -.

CHAPTER 1

BACKGROUNDS

1. A Short History of Ostia

1.1. The earliest period

According to some ancient authors, Ostia, which means Mouth (of the Tiber), was founded by Ancus Marcius, the fourth king of Rome. He supposedly reigned from 640 to 616 BC. The foundation of the *urbs* (city) or *colonia* perhaps took place around 620 BC. Archaeological evidence for such an early date, however, is absent. Possibly the settlement was located at another spot as formerly the Tiber had a different course, debouching near Fiumicino, now the location of Rome's airport. A settlement may have existed there for as early as the Middle and Late Bronze Age (ca 1700-1000 BC). Salt from large salt beds (*salinae*) was transported to Rome and from there along the prehistoric predecessor of the Via Salaria (Salt Way) to the central regions of Italy. In the winter nomadic shepherds descended from the mountains to the coasts of Etruria and Latium in order to collect salt. They returned to the grassy mountains in the summer.

Ostia's rulers and inhabitants in the imperial period may have believed that their city was founded by Ancus Marcius. A reused marble tablet from a sewer under the Via dei Molini, dated to the second century AD, carries the following inscription (*CIL* XIV S 4338):

A[NCO]	
MAR[CIO]	
REG[I …]	
QUART[O A R]OMULO	*For Ancus Marcius, the fourth king*
QUI A[B URBE C]ONDIT[A]	*after Romulus, who, after the foun-*
[PRI]MUM COLONI[AM]	*dation of the city (Rome) first*
[---] DEDUX[IT]	*founded the colony (Ostia)*

The text may refer to a statue of the king, placed on the Forum or in a sanctuary.

The Republican rectangular fortification, usually called *castrum*, was built around 300 BC. Livy describes it as a *colonia maritima*, a colony on the sea. The date is based on Etrusco-Campanian sherds recovered from the lowest level of the *fossae* (ditches) in which the *castrum* walls were built. These walls consist of rectangular tuff blocks. Some were preserved, because after the Second Punic War, when they lost their defensive function, they were used as rear walls of buildings. There must have been a sanctuary by the 5th or 4th century BC in view of architectonic ornaments and terracotta antefixes. Imported Attic, Etruscan, and Faliscan redfigure vase sherds date to the 4th century BC. These artefacts were found in the area of the (later) *castrum*. Ostia was dependent on Rome, governed by a *quaestor Ostiensis* after 267 BC.

After the Punic Wars the import of grain from Sicily and Sardinia intensified. Probably under Tiberius Gracchus (ca 130 BC) a space to the east of the *castrum* along the Tiber, along the north side of the main east-west street (*decumanus*), was earmarked for storing grain. The inscriptions on four travertine boundary stones describe the area as public (*ager publicus*). Between 63 and 58 BC Ostia was provided with a long city wall (formerly called Sullan walls) with three main gates, now called Porta Romana, Porta Laurentina and Porta Marina, on the initiative of the famous orator Cicero. Between 63 and 49 BC Ostia gained independence from Rome. The oldest (reused) fragment of the marble *Fasti Ostienses*, the local yearly calendar listing the names of the most important magistrates and events in Rome and Ostia, dates to 49 BC. Cicero (*Pro Murena* 8.18) describes the *provincia ostiensis* as an unpleasant environment: *non tam gratiosam et illustrem quam negotiosam et molestam* (not so much gracious and famous as busy and uncomfortable).

Few buildings of the Republican period remain: the temples in the Sacred Area of the Hercules temple (see no 21), the Four Small Temples to the west of the Theatre (see no 9) and some atrium-houses (see no 35). Most old buildings lie beneath the 2nd century AD city, and a few in the area to the east of the *castrum*.

1.2. Growth and boom

The first public buildings date to the Julio-Augustan period. The theatre, the oldest stone one outside Rome, was built just before 17 BC. The Temple of Roma and Augustus, to the south of the Forum, is now dated to the reign of Augustus, ca AD 10. The town council made decisions there (*CIL* XIV 353). As the Tiber was not very accessible to sea ships from Egypt, North Africa, Sicily and Sardinia, and as grain and other goods were mainly transferred over land from the harbour of Puteoli (Pozzuoli) to Rome, two new artificial harbours were constructed in swift succession, ca 3 km northwest of Ostia. The space between these harbours and Ostia is called Isola Sacra in Italian (Sacred Island, also called Island of Venus (*insula Veneris*)). *Portus Augusti*, the first, large sea harbour with two curved piers near Fiumicino, was initiated by Claudius in AD 42 and finished by Nero in AD 64. Claudius furthermore constructed a canal from the Tiber to the harbour: 'to free the city (Rome) from inundations'. A heavy storm revealed that the port was not a safe haven. Therefore, Trajan built a second, hexagonal, inner harbour between 110 and 112. Together, the harbours were called *Portus uterque* (Both Harbours). Seaships departed and arrived between March and October. Under Constantine Portus became an independent city: *civitas Flavia Constantiniana Portuensis*. A canal (*Fossa Traiana*) linked the harbours with the Tiber. Small tug-boats transferred grain and other goods to Rome and to Ostia. A *procurator annonae* was responsible for the grain supply. He was subordinate to the *praefectus annonae* in Rome.

The oldest granaries in Ostia date to the Republican period (see e.g. no 41). In the second half of the 1st century AD a successful middle class emerged, consisting mainly of freedmen (*liberti*). In inscriptions they can be identified by their third, Latinized Greek name (*cognomen*). Hardworking slaves from the Greek-speaking Mediterranean part of the Roman empire easily integrated into the society; they learned Latin and were freed and often also adopted by their patrons. Descendants of freedmen usually remained recognizable by their non-Roman surname.

The same period saw the birth of the first so-called guilds, clubs of men who shared the same profession or interest. A guild, called *corpus* or *collegium* in Latin, needed an initial permission for gathering from the Senate in Rome for political safety reasons. It had a clubhouse (*schola*) where members could recline, eat and drink, celebrate birthdays and worship Roman emperors. Some guilds had a temple, dedicated to the tutelary deity of the guild or profession. In the 2nd century guilds formed the social backbone of Ostia. Guilds consisted of *patroni* (honorary patrons), *magistri quinquennales* (presidents for five years) or *magistri perpetui* (for life) and *plebs* (common members).

Under Domitian, around 96, large parts of Ostia were raised by about one meter, probably as a measure against inundations. The first large flat buildings (*insulae*), called Casette Tipo in Italian, date to the reign of the next emperor, Trajan. An enormous building boom took place under Hadrian (117-138) who twice held the position of one of the two annual mayors of the city. Large areas in the centre, in the west (Garden Houses/ Case a giardino (120-125)) and in the former *ager publicus* saw the construction of new buildings (126-138). In the 120s, the Capitolium (*CIL* XIV 32), probably dedicated to Jupiter, Juno and Minerva, was built in the centre. The preferred building technique style was *opus reticulatum mixtum*, a network of tuff layers with brick quoins. Towards the end of and after Hadrian's reign, the masonry was usually in brick (*opus latericium*). After ca 250 *opus reticulatum* was incidentally used once again.

In the many new flats and apartment buildings, successful members of the middle class, usually freedmen, lived on the ground floor. The less fortunate hired the upper floors; usually their only access was via external, travertine staircases. Both groups of inhabitants, however, may have shared water and cult facilities in buildings which had a central, open court. Most buildings featured rooms along the streetside, which were used as shops, workshops or bars (*tabernae*). They could be closed by means of wooden doors sliding in the grooves in travertine thresholds. The total number of *tabernae* amounts to some 800! Until recently, the total number of inhabitants in the 2nd century AD was estimated at around 60.000. Recent geophysical research in the form of magnetometry and ground penetrating radar has however made clear that the city had large quarters outside the Ciceronian walls. In addition, the population number may have been flexible due to the grain trade season in spring and summer.

After Hadrian's reign building activities diminished slightly but still new flats, baths and temples were built. The Theatre was enlarged under Commodus and Septimius Severus (see no 6). The 2nd century was the period during which oriental deities like Serapis (see no 26), Cybele (no 37) and Mithras (after ca 160; see nos 22 and 40) became popular, probably because they offered hope of salvation or a life after death. The Jews converted a building along the Via Severiana, near the ancient seashore, beyond the city walls, ca 500 m to the southeast of Porta Marina, into a synagogue between ca AD 50 and 100. A bilingual inscription (with one line in Latin and the other in Greek (*SEG* 51, 1414)) on a marble slab from the second half of the 2nd century, reused in the floor of the vestibule (the original is in the local museum), begins with the words: PRO SALVTE AVG[G](vstorvm) (for the well-being of the emperors). The semicircular shrine in the Synagogue originally contained the chest with the scrolls of the Torah. It is oriented towards Jerusalem. Two corbels of marble architraves exhibit the typical Jewish symbols: *menorah* (candelabrum with seven arms), *lulav* (palm leaf), *ethrog* (lemon) and *shofar* (horn). One original is now exposed near the local museum. The last pagan temple, the

Round Temple (Tempio Rotondo) near the Forum, possibly dedicated to the cult of emperors, is dated to ca AD 235.

1.3. Decline and a short revival

The 3rd century gradually evolved into a period of crisis for the Roman Empire. There were many military emperors who reigned for only a short period. No cohorts of firemen are mentioned in inscriptions after 239 (see no 5). The most recent statue base on the Square of the Guilds (Piazzale delle Corporazioni) dates to 249 (see no 7, base no 6) and that on the Campus of the Magna Mater to 256 (see no 37). The last mention of a *pontifex Volkani*, high priest of the firegod Vulcanus (see below), dates to 251. The *Augustales*, successful freedmen who were dignitaries of the cult of Augustus and later emperors, are mentioned for the last time in the 250s. The last temple, the Round Temple near the Forum, was probably finished around 244. Some buildings that had caught fire were not restored. *Portus Uterque* evidently became more important than Ostia. Members of the elite, however, converted apartment buildings with windows into aristocratic houses (*domus*), with a slightly raised hall (*aula*) in the rear which functioned as a reception hall. These houses, now without windows for reasons of security, were decorated with marble and splendid mosaics. The most luxurious mosaics are in the *aulae* (reception halls), in *opus sectile*, made of cut slabs of marble in different colours. Some *domus* have a little garden (*viridarium*) with a water fountain (*nymphaeum*). The most luxurious have internal baths. Names of owners are not known but it seems likely that not only the local elite but also members of the Senate in Rome and high officials involved in the grain supply enjoyed the pleasant sea climate in the quiet city. Striking for this period is the use of *spolia*, building elements, bases and even gravestones from elsewhere, which were recycled. Some streets were closed in the third and later centuries because of their dirtiness (see no 16). On the other hand some splendid marble water fountains (*nymphaea*) were built along the main streets. They were meant to suggest, like a Potemkin façade, the impression of a prosperous city. In these centuries a new building technique appeared, perhaps due to a crisis in the brick industries around Rome: *opus vittatum*, or alternating horizontal bands of brick and tuff. While Christian religion was tolerated in 313 and though Ostia had a bishop (Maximus), the city seems to have been mainly pagan until ca 394. The Basilica of Constantine, dedicated to the blessed apostles Petrus, Paul and John mentioned in the *Liber Pontificalis* (33.28-29), has recently been discovered thanks to German geophysical research inside the city walls, near the small city gate between Porta Romana and Porta Laurentina. Its peripheral position suggests that Christian religion was not dominant in the 4th century.

As late as the period between AD 375 and 420 the city received several facelifts, among others porticoes, marble *nymphaea* (fountains), and restorations of baths (*CIL* XIV 137). The Macellum (Meat market) was repaired by Aurelius Anicius Symmachus, prefect of Rome and member of a renowned pagan, aristocratic family (*CIL* XIV S 4719). The three most recent *domus*, all of considerable dimensions, also date to this period. Prefects of the grain supply played an important role in this last prosperous period (see nos 6 and 16). The 6th century author Cassiodorus (*Variae epistulae* 7.9) was impressed both by Ostia and Portus. He called them *ornatissimas civitates* (most splendid cities).

The last buildings to be built were some small baths, at the beginning of the 6th century. During the course of the 6th century the aqueduct fell into disuse, after which wells were dug and well-heads made, even in the middle of streets, including in the *decumanus*. Due to the raids of the Saracenes the last few inhabitants abandoned Ostia in the 9th century.

Pilgrims, however, continued to visit the shrine of a martyr, Cyriacus, built near the Theatre in the 6th or 7th century. Cyriacus was bishop in the 3rd century. He was killed, together with Aurea, in front of Caracalla's Arch (of AD 216), which was connected to the Theatre and bridged the *decumanus*. The inscription on the (now missing) lid of a sarcophagus in the oratory depicting Orpheus (*AE* 1910, 202) reads: HIC QVIRIACVS DORMIT IN PACE (here Quiriacus rests in peace). Quiriacus may be Cyriacus.

In 1557 the Tiber changed its course (see cover folder and map pp. X-XI). The river overran part of the city in *Regio* I, the area to the north-east of the Capitolium.

2. THE POLITICAL ORGANISATION OF OSTIA

In the Republican period Ostia was governed by a high official from Rome, first a *quaestor*, later a *praetor*. Probably in or soon after 63 BC, the city became an independent *colonia* (called *colonia ostiensis* or *ostiensium*, *res publica ostiensis*, *Ostia* and in late antiquity *Hostia*) and it was provided with large city walls. The inhabitants were called *Ostienses* (Ostians) or *coloni*. Two mayors (*duumviri* or *duoviri*: 'two men') were the highest officials for one year. They were protected by two *lictores*. The latter marched in front of them holding *fasces* (iron rods, symbols of power).

The mayors were assisted by *aediles*. The *quaestor aerarii* was responsible for the finances, the *aediles* for infrastructure, especially the markets and the public order. The *ordo decurionum* (class of the *decuriones*), town council, comprised 100 *decuriones* who were elected by co-option (*allectio*). The minimum age was 25 but in later centuries even 12-year-old boys could become members. Men with special merits could be elected *gratis* (or *gratuitus*), that is without paying an 'entrance fee'. Men with a successful career or with special merits could become *patroni*. A *patronus*, the highest honorary official, defended the public cause of Ostia in the Senate of Rome. Scribes assisted officials and the town council. The latter approved the placing of statues in public spaces (see no 7). New magistrates in the 2nd century AD were the *quaestor alimentorum*, who managed the charity fund for children, and the *curator operum publicorum et aquarum*, who was responsible for public buildings and water facilities. The *praefectus annonae*, chief of the grain supply, was *curator rei publicae Ostiensium*, curator of Ostia city, after ca 250. After ca 350 he was subordinate to the *praefectus urbi*, chief of Rome.

In religious matters the *pontifex Volkani et aedium sacrarum* ('the high priest of Vulcanus and sacred buildings'), held the highest function, probably for life. His title occurs only in Ostian inscriptions. He controlled activities in all sanctuaries, such as the placing of statues (see no 37). He was assisted by the *aediles sacris Volkani faciundis* (assistents in the sacred things or acts of (for) Vulcanus). Priesthoods were part of the *cursus honorum* (path of honours), in other words the career path of all public and religious functions. No sanctuary or temple of Vulcanus has been found so far. It was probably located outside the city walls. An inscription that reads *Volcano sacrum* (*AE* 1986, 114) has been found near the Synagogue, in the suburban southwest area of the excavation terrain. Vitruvius (*De architectura* 7.30.13-21) states that according to the religious books of Etruscan *haruspices* ('seers'), temples for Venus, Volcanus and Mars had to be built outside the city because of the dangers of lust, fire and war. Interestingly, at Herculaneum a temple for Vulcanus, Minerva, Neptunus and Mercurius is indeed situated *extra muros*. An urban temple of Volcanus may have been situated in the region of the Theatre (*AE* 1986, 115; Reg. V, ii, 6).

Other important priests in Ostia were the *sacerdos genii coloniae* (priest of the tutelary deity (*genius*) of the *colonia*) and the *Augustales*. In the 2nd and 3rd centuries these priests, usually freedmen, were called *seviri Augustales* (six men for the emperor cult). They may have served in the temple of Roma and Augustus, to the south of the Forum, which was built around AD 10.

CHAPTER 2

IN SITU INSCRIPTIONS

1. The Statue Base for the Well-Being of Caesar Augustus

At the western end of Ostia's cemetery along the *Via Ostiensis*, to the right of the street near the city's main gate, now called Porta Romana (*fig. 1*), there is a large marble statue base with an inscription on the side facing the street (*CIL* XIV S 4324; *fig. 2*):

SALUTI CAESARIS AUGUST(i)
GLABRIO PATRONUS COLONIAE D(ono) D(edit) F(aciendum) C(uravit)

For the Well-being of Caesar Augustus. Glabrio, patron of the colonia *(Ostia), has given (this) as gift (and) and has taken care of (this)*

This dedicatory inscription was made by a man who held the highest honorary title in Ostia: *patronus*. He was patron and protector of the city. One could only receive the title from the town council. Because he had to promote the public cause of the city, usually a high official from Rome was elected. The abbreviation DD is problematic. One of the alternative readings is *d(ecreto) d(ecurionum)* (by decree of the town council). In favour of *dono* or *donum dedit*, however, is the fact that many inscriptions mention the formula *de sua pecunia faciendum curavit* (with his own money he had it made). Assuming that *de sua pecunia* has been left out carelessly, we may suppose that Glabrio himself would have paid for the monument.

The marble base is situated in a strategic place, at the entrance of Ostia's most important city gate. Everybody arriving from Rome had to pass it. The inscription probably dates to the reign of the emperor Augustus. Tiberius, Claudius and Nero may be ruled out as inscriptions elsewhere mention *pro salute Tiberi Caesaris* (*AE* 1923, 10), *pro salute Tiberi Claudi Caesaris Augusti* (*AE* 1985, 392), and *pro salute Neronis Claudi* (*AE* 1980, 656), without the initial title Caesar Augustus. In addition, from Nero onwards, inscriptions mention *pro salute imp(eratoris)* and the name of the emperor.

Fig. 1. Porta Romana, statue base and boundary stone (photo author).

Fig. 2. Statue base for the Well-being of Caesar Augustus (photo author).

Manius Acilius Glabrio, who was *consul suffectus* (elect) in 33 and *proconsul* (governor) of Africa in 25 BC, may have dedicated the base and its statue in 16 BC when Augustus was likely ill. On a coin dated 16 BC we read *Senatus consulto ob republicam cum salute imperatoris Caesaris Augusti conservatam* ((coined) by decree of the Senate because of the preservation of the Republic with the health of the Emperor Caesar Augustus). *Salus* can mean health or safety.

The *Acilii Glabriones* had had a close relation with the deified personification *Salus* since the 3rd century BC. A *denarius* of 49 BC coined by a Manius Acilius depicts a female head with the inscription *Salutis* (of Safety) on the reverse and on the obverse *Valetudo* (Health), a standing woman leaning on a column who holds a snake in her right hand. The family may have been responsible for or associated with the *Compitum Acilium* or *Compitum Acili*, a shrine at a crossroads in the centre of Rome. According to Pliny (*Naturalis Historia* 29.12) the first Greek physician who worked in Rome, Archagathus from the Peloponnesus, opened a medical shop there in 219 BC. He was a radical doctor, surnamed *carnifex* (the butcher!), but appreciated. He became a Roman citizen.

A statue of *Salus* may have stood on the base, facing the street. Imperial coins with the inscription SALUS or SALUS AUG(usti), from the time of Nero onwards, show her initially as a woman sitting on a throne with a shallow dish in her right hand and later standing and holding a dish from which a snake is about to drink. In many inscriptions this personification, called *Hygieia* (Health) in Greek, is mentioned together with Aesculapius, the Greek Asklepios, the healing god. Two aligned corroded iron pegs on the base's surface, may indicate the original position of two legs of the throne or the feet of the female statue.

It is less likely that the base supported a statue of the emperor, as men's feet were not placed side-by-side in a straight line.

The base is placed on a marble block which rests on two layers of three blocks of travertine. The combination of marble and travertine is also found in two Mausolea near the ancient shoreline outside Porta Marina, dated to ca 30-20 BC (see nos 28 and 29) and in the Theatre, dated to ca 17 BC (see no 6). These dates confirm the proposed date of the base.

The *Acilii Glabriones* remained powerful in Rome until the 5th century AD (see no 8). Several of them were consuls (see no 8 and *CIL* XIV 250). One became consul in 124, his son in 152, and his grandson in 186.

In front of the base, to the right, the most easterly of four travertine stones marks the southern boundary of the ca 600 m (ca 2000 Roman feet) long *ager publicus* (public domain), between the Tiber and the *decumanus* (east-west main street). As the inscription on the small stone is barely preserved, one of the better preserved large stones will be dealt with later on (see no 12).

2. The Inscriptions of Porta Romana

Behind the remaining part of the main city gate, on the left, plaster copies of two large marble tablets with very incomplete, probably almost identical inscriptions, are attached to the city wall (*fig. 3*); the original, marble fragments are now missing. Originally, they were placed in the upper part of the gate, one at the front and one at the back, about ten metres above street level. The inscriptions have been reconstructed by F. Zevi and others (*AE* 1997, 253):

SE[NATUS P]OPULU[SQUE ROMANUS]
C[OLON]IA[E OSTIEN]SIUM M[U]RO[S] ET PORTAS DED[IT]
M(arcus) [TULLIUS CICER]O C[OS FECIT CURA]VIT[QUE
P(ublius) CL[ODIU]S P[U]LCHE[R TR(ibunus) PL(ebis) CON]SUM-
MAVIT PROBAVIT
P[ORTAM VETUS]TATE [C]ORRUPTA[M---][OSTIENSES?]---[OMNI
DECOR)]E A [SOLO]--[REFECE]RU[NT]

The Senate and the People of Rome have given the walls and gates of the colonia *of the inhabitants of Ostia. Marcus Tullius Cicero, consul, made and oversaw (them). Publius Clodius Pulcher, tribune of the people, completed and approved (them). The gate, affected by old age (obj.), [the Ostians (subj.)] [with all decoration from the bottom up (?) have remade] (> The Ostians restored the gate, affected by the tooth of time, with all its decoration, from its foundations (?))*

Restituerunt is also possible instead of the reconstructed *refecerunt*.

The inscriptions are dated around AD 100 in view of the style of the architectural marble decoration of the rebuilt gate. The first part of the text, up to the words *portam vetustate corruptam*, copies older inscriptions. Following a decree of the Senate, Cicero, the famous orator, took the initiative to build the city walls in 63 BC. The builder was probably his friend, Sicca, chief of the builders. The notorious Claudius Pulcher, called Clodius by the rabble, completed the monument in 58 BC. In the night of the 4th of December 62 BC he participated in a nocturnal feast in honour of Bona Dea (Good Goddess) at Caesar's house, a happening that was strictly for-

Fig. 3. Inscription from the Porta Romana (photo author).

bidden for men. He tried to seduce Caesar's wife Pompeia there. In the ensuing religious trial in 61 BC he was prosecuted but acquitted by corrupt jurymen. So Cicero and Clodius became enemies. In reaction to this, Clodius may have annexed Cicero's building project. Cicero's initiative may have implied that Ostia became independent from Rome in 63 BC, becoming a *colonia* and getting its own town council. City walls were necessary since Ostia had been plundered by consul Marius in 87 BC and attacked by sea pirates in 67 BC. As the political situation in 58 BC was not stable, the city walls may have been completed later on, in the 50s BC. The city walls may have been used as an aqueduct in AD 77/78 under the reign of Vespasian. Ostia's first aqueduct, which ended up in a large cistern to the south of Porta Romana, was built under Tiberius (AD 34) and probably finished under Caligula or Claudius.

3. THE BATHS OF THE CHARIOT DRIVERS (TERME DEI CISIARII; II, ii, 3)

To the north of Ostia's main street, the *decumanus* (the extension of the Via Ostiensis), there are remains of several buildings, on a far lower level. The tuff pillars of an old *porticus*, reused in later buildings, date to the Republican period. Most impressive is a private bath complex (*balneum*), dated between ca AD 110 and 130, built on the remains of a Republican court building with shops. Almost in front of the modern street, which leads to the museum, there is a cold water-room (*frigidarium*) with a fascinating, black-and-white mosaic. The centre of the mosaic schematically depicts the old Republican *castrum*-walls with four gates. The towers in the four corners and the walls are supported by *telamones*/atlants, mythical giants. Between them, two-weeled chariots are visible, each drawn by one or two mules. They show four stages in the transport of persons. Along the borders of the mosaic the Ciceronian city walls might be depicted, although these did not form a square. The mules have nicknames. The names of the animals led by reins by a man (without chariot) are (*CIL* XIV S 4754; *fig. 4*):

PUDES (Pudens) PO /   *Modest/bashful*
DAGROSUS (Podagrosus)   *Gouty*

The second mule, Podagrosus, stretches his hind leg which is evidently affected by gout.

In the next scene a passenger leaves the chariot using little stairs. In the meantime two mules are fed. Their names are (*fig. 5*):

POTISCUS   BAROSUS   *Thirsty   Stupid (effeminate, soft)*

The adjective *potiscus* may derive from *potus* ('drink'). The rare adjective *barosus* is only explained in the *Glossarium Philoxeni*. Potiscus and Barosus were also used as personal surnames (*cognomina*).

The other two scenes, without inscriptions, show the transport of passengers. A couple of seahorses, led by Neptune, the sea god holding his trident and moving a billowing veil, along with mixed creatures with fish-tails, dolphins and swimming men signal the function of the room.

The mosaics have much in common with those in the Baths of Neptune and the Baths of the Seven Wise Man (see no 23), which also date to the Hadrianic period, probably to ca 120.
It is likely that the same artisans made them.

A fragment of another black-and-white mosaic in the southern room with an apse shows a nude athlete holding what looks like a *strigilis* in his raised right hand (*fig. 6*). A strigil is an instrument to cleanse the body of oil and dirt after boxing or wrestling. The unpublished Greek inscription above him reads: KPEIKON[---] / PEICEK[---], in transcription: Kreikon

Fig. 4. Mosaic in the Baths of the Cisiarii. Detail (photo author).

Fig. 5. Mosaic in the Baths of the Cisiarii. Detail (photo author).

Fig. 6. Mosaic in the Baths of the Cisiarii. Detail (photo author).

[---] / reise k[---]). It may be reconstructed as *Kreikon enereise* or *katereise kaloos*, which means: Kreikon pushed (his opponent) down nicely. Exclamations are not uncommon on mosaics. An athlete on a mosaic in Rome for example exclaims A LAPONI VICTUS ES (Ah La(m)ponius, you are conquered!). Athletes are also represented in mosaics of other Ostian baths. *Palaestrae* (wrestling spaces) may have been used by traveling sportsmen from the eastern, Greek-speaking part of the Roman Empire (see no 31), but also by Roman aficionados.

These baths were probably owned by the guild of ancient 'cab'-drivers. Thus its bathers were probably members of the guild. In Latin two-wheeled chariots are called *cisia* (plural of *cisium*). *Cisiarii* is the Latin word for coachmen. An inscription with a list of guilds (*CIL* XIV 409) mentions *iuvenes cisiani*; it is, therefore, likely that these men had a professional union. It can be no coincidence that these baths lie not far from the Porta Romana. From there one could travel along the *Via Ostiensis* to Rome. Perhaps the *cisiarii* were bound to the territory of Ostia. An inscription found in front of the Porta di Stabia at Pompeii (*CIL* X 1064) dated to the beginning of the 1st century, mentioning the consolidation of a street gives an indication of this: ... *a milliario ad cisarios qua territorium est*

Fig. 7. Mosaic in the Bar of Fortunatus (photo author).

Pompeianorum… (… from the milestone (near the gate) to the coachmen where the territory of the Pompeians ends…).

4. THE BAR OF FORTUNATUS (CAUPONA DI FORTUNATO; II, vi, 1)

The bar situated near the crossroads of the *decumanus* and the Street of the Fountain, which leads to the Barracks of the Firemen, features a black-and-white mosaic with a damaged inscription (*CIL* XIV S 4756; *fig. 7*):

[HOSPES INQUIT] FORTUNATUS
[VINUM E CR]ATERA QUOD SITIS
    BI   BE

['Guest', says] Fortunatus: ['wine from the cr]ater, because you are thirsty, drink!'

Between BI and BE a *crater* is illustrated. A *crater* was used to mix wine and water.

In antiquity wine was not commonly drunk pure. The mosaic is dated to the first half of the 4th century AD. The barkeeper had chosen a strategic location for his bar. No remains of a stone counter have survived.

The inscription can only be read from the entrance on the east side where a small street runs past the bar.

5. The Barracks of the Firemen (Caserma dei Vigili; II, v, 1)

Augustus or Tiberius first stationed a *cohors praetoria* ('cohort of the imperial guard') at Ostia. One of the soldiers died while trying to extinguish a fire. He received a public funeral and a tomb in the cemetery near Porta Romana (*CIL* XIV S 4494). Claudius posted a cohort of soldier-firefighters (*vigiles*: 'watchmen'), *sebarii* or *sebaciarii* ('night-watchmen') to Puteoli (modern Pozzuoli) and Ostia around AD 50 (Suetonius, *Claudius* 25.2). The first stone barracks (*kastra/castra*) in Ostia, initiated by the emperor Domitian (AD 90), were not finished by him, probably because he fell in disgrace. The foundations and a lead water pipe inscribed with the word *castra* lie under the present building, which was built under Hadrian (126-138). It was inaugurated around 138. It is a rectangular building with many rooms grouped around a rectangular open court, with water basins in two corners. It was repaired in 200. It shows the keen interest of emperors taken in the protection of the Ostian granaries and public order. Staircases, which are accessible from the exterior of the building, prove the existence of at least one, but probably more upper floors.

The firemen stayed in Ostia for four months. They were replaced by colleagues from Rome, from all seven cohorts successively. One *cohors* consisted of 7 *centuriae* of 70 to 80 men. One *vexillatio*, detached for four months, comprised 4 *centuriae* (ca 300 men). The firemen patrolled day and night on a rotating basis. Those who were not on patrol partook in exercises, slept or repaired materials: buckets, fire-blankets, brooms for the extinction of small fires and ladders. Whoever noticed a fire, shouted: *aqua* ('water!'). Vitruvius describes a *ctesibica machina*, a pump, called after his inventor Ktesibos and used by the firemen. If demolition was called for, stakes, hooks attached to ropes and pick-axes or axes were used. Houses adjacent to burning premises were often demolished in order to prevent a larger fire. In case of fire the firemen formed a line. Water from a fountain or cistern was poured into buckets which were passed down the line and thrown on the fire or in the pump reservoir. Vinegar was used as a chemical means of extinguishing. Enormous city fires like that in Rome under Nero, in AD 64, are hardly known for Ostia. The *Fasti Ostienses* mention a fire in AD 115 which destroyed several properties, probably in one city quarter (*vicus*). It appears that the Great Bakery along the Street of the Milling Stones suffered a great fire in the 3rd century AD. It was not rebuilt, probably due to the fact that Ostia became less important than Portus.

The barracks contain sleeping- and storerooms, offices and a latrine. In the western part, facing the eastern main gate, is the *Caesareum* or *Augusteum* (fig. 8), a sacred space where the chief commander (*praefectus*), cohorts, commanders of a cohort (*tribuni*) or detachment (*praepositi*), and *centuriones* (chiefs of a *centuria*) placed statues of their emperors.

The black-and-white mosaic in the vestibule (now covered) shows three phases of the slaughter of a bull (*taurobolium*), a sacrifice in honour of deified emperors.

In the *Caesareum* and the adjacent part of the court there are fourteen inscribed statue bases, dedicated to emperors and their relatives. Fragments of other bases have been found nearby, and some bases ended up in the mediaeval lime kilns. The in situ bases date to the period AD 137 until 241-244. The most recent in situ base is dedicated to Furia Sabina, wife of the emperor Gordian. A slender statue base in the Round Temple (Tempio Rotondo; I, ii, 1) to the southwest of the Forum, mentions her too: *F[uriae Sab]iniae / Tranquill[inae] / [---]* (for Furia Sabinia Tranquillina; *NSc* 1927, 394, no 25).

Fig. 8. Statue bases in the Barracks of the Firemen (photo author).

The marble bases on the podium, which has stairs on its north side, mention emperors of the 2nd century, from left to right:

1. Marcus Aurelius (AD 140-145, not yet emperor; *CIL* XIV S 4366)
2. Marcus Aurelius (AD 162; *CIL* XIV S 4368)
3. L. Septimius Severus (AD 195; *CIL* XIV S 4380)
4. L. Aurelius Verus (AD 162; *CIL* XIV S 4376)
5. Antoninus Pius (AD 138; *CIL* XIV S 4357)

It is evident that Septimius Severus is the main figure, symmetrically flanked by predecessors.

The limestone base on the ground to the right (north side) of the podium records:
6. Lucius Aelius, adoptive son of Hadrianus (AD 137; *CIL* XIV S 4356)

The marble bases in the court record emperors or their wives of the third century, from left to right:
7. Caracalla (4 April AD 211 (his birthday); *CIL* XIV S 4388)
8. Gordian III (4 February AD 239 (not his birthday); CIL XIV S 4397)
9. Furia Sabina, Gordian's wife (AD 241-244; *CIL* XIV S 4398)
10. Septimius Severus (AD 207; *CIL* XIV S 4381)
11. No text, inscription erased; it may have mentioned Geta because he received a *damnatio memoriae* (damnation of memory) in AD 211.
12. Septimius Severus (AD 207; *CIL* XIV S 4387)
13. Iulia (Domna), wife of Septimius Severus (AD 193-217); *CIL* XIV S 4386)
14. M. [[Opellius]]. Antoninus [[Diadumenianus]] (AD 217; *CIL* XIV S 4393), son of *Imperator Caesar*. M. Opellius Severus Macrinus was responsible for the murder of Caracalla in 217. Opelllius Antoninus died in 218.

Base 6, the oldest, is made of limestone, so it may have been transferred from elsewhere. The others are made of white marble. Some bases can be dated precisely to one particular year, thanks to the presence of the names of two consuls. Base 7 mentions names of consuls on the left side, and base 8 on the right. Interestingly, base 7 was placed on the birthday of Caracalla (compare *CIL* XIV S 4389, a fragmentary marble tablet, also found in the Barracks). There is no base for Commodus (AD 180-192) because he received a *damnatio memoriae*, like Geta on base 11 and Opellius on base 14. The damnation by Senate decree implied erasing the name of a hated person from inscriptions, and destroying, burying, decapitating or damaging statues of him or his representations on reliefs, paintings, and coins. Sometimes the erasing was done rather carelessly, so that letters still remain legible.

Below are three texts and translations.

Base 2:

IMP(eratori) CAESARI
DIVI ANTONINI FILIO
DIVI HADRIANI NEPOTI
DIVI TRAIANI PRONEP(oti)
DIVI NERVAE ABNEPOTI
M(arco) AURELIO ANTONINO AUG(usto)
PONT(ifici) MAX(imo) TRIB(unicia) POT(estate) $\overline{XVI}$ CO(n)S(uli) $\overline{III}$
COHORTES VII VIG(ilum)

For Imperator Caesar Marcus Aurelius Antoninus Augustus, son of the divine Antoninus, grandson of the divine Hadrian, great-grandson of the divine Trajan, great-great-grandson of the divine Nerva, high-priest, sixteen times endowed with the power of tribune of the people, three times consul. Seven cohorts of firefighters.

Base 3 (*fig. 9*):

IMP(eratori) L(ucio) SEPTIMIO SE /
VERO PERTINACI
CAESARI AUG(usto)
PONT(ifici) MAX(maximo) TRIB(unicia) POT(estate) $\overline{III}$
IMP(eratori) $\overline{V}$ CO(n)S(uli) $\overline{II}$ PRO CO(n)S(uli) P(atri) P(atriae)
COHORTES.$\overline{VII}$ VIG(ilum)
[[FULVIO PLAUTIANO]] PRAEF(ecto) VIG(ilum) CASSIO
LIGURE TRIBUNO PRAEPOSITO VEXILLATIONIS

For Imperator Emperor Lucius Septimius Severus Pertinax Augustus, high-priest, three times endowed with the power of tribune of the people, five times Imperator, thrice consul, proconsul, *father of the fatherland. Seven cohorts of firefighters, when (Fulvius Plautianus, name erased) was commander of the firefighters and Cassius Ligus chief of a detachment.*

Both bases depict a wine pitcher in low relief on the left side and a *patera*

Fig. 9. Statue base in the Barracks of the Firemen (photo author).

Fig. 10. Statue base in the Barracks of the Firemen (photo author).

umbilicata (dish with navel) on the right, symbolizing the offering of wine. On the upper edge of the front side are reliefs showing *bucrania* (bullheads), a *lituus* (curved priest staff), a wine pitcher, a *patera umbilicata*, and a torch: clear references to the emperor cult and the offering of bulls. The inscription for Marcus Aurelius on base 2 dates to AD 162 and that for Septimius Severus on base 3 to 195. It may imply that the front of base 3 was blank until 195, and that the sculptor of base 3 copied the reliefs from base 2. But as Septimius Severus is the central, main person on the podium, it cannot be ruled out that base 2 was made 33 years after 162. The title *pater patriae* was first used by Augustus in 2 BC. Earlier, in 44 BC, Caesar received the title *parens patriae* ('father of the fatherland').

The inscription on base 13 reads (*fig. 10*):

    IULIAE
      AUG(ustae)
MATRI AUGUSTI (second I in superscript)
ET KASTRORUM
SUB CN(aeo) M(arco) RUSTIO RUFINO PR(aefecto) VIG(ilum) E(minentissimo) V(iro)
CURANTIBUS
C(aio) LAECANIO NOVATILLIANO SUB PR(aefecto) ET
M(arco) FL(avio) RAESIANO TRIB(uno) COH(ortis) II VIG(ilum)
    PRAEPOSITO VEXILLATIONIS

For Julia Augusta, mother of the emperor and the barracks, under Gnaeus Marcus Rustius Rufinus, commander of the firefighters, a very eminent man. Thanks to the care of Gaius Laecanius Novatillianus, deputy-commander, and Marcus Flavius Raesianus, chief of the second cohort of the firefighters, chief of the detachment

The empress Julia Domna was the wife of the emperor Septimius Severus from AD 180 onwards and mother of Geta and Caracalla. She was honoured as patron of the Barracks (compare *CIL* XIV 120, 123-124). The last characters of the word *curantibus* are, as on base 11 and 12, incised on an erased, lower level. Probably the scribe intended to write *curam agentibus*, changed his mind, and changed *curam* into *curantibus*.

    Some graffiti, written by firemen, are visible on the right wall of the *Caesareum* and elsewhere in the Barracks.

    In addition, marble tablets, found nearby (not in situ), mention names of firefighters who received FP: *frumentum publicum* ('public bread') on a specific day (*CIL* XIV S 4499-4508).

In the southeast corner of the Barracks there is a large latrine. It has an inscribed, marble altar and an inscribed, little chapel (*aedicula*), inserted high in the wall. Both are now only visible through a closed fence.

The inscription on the altar reads (*CIL* XIV S 4281):

C(aius) VALERIUS
MYRON B(ene)F(iciarius) PR (aefecti)
COH(ortis) IIII VIG(ilum)
FORTUNAE
SANCTAE
V(otum) S(olvit) L(ibens) M(erito)

Gaius Valerius Myron, beneficiarius of the chief of the fourth cohort of the firefighters
has kept his promise to Sacred Fortuna, gladly and with pleasure

The pediment of the *aedicula* holds a short text (*CIL* XIV S 4282):

FORTUNAE SANCT(ae)   *For Sacred Fortuna*

The latrine was conceived as a sacred place for Fortuna, personification and goddess of luck. The dedication was based on the principle *do ut des*: I give in the hope that you give. The believer closed his prayer with a legal contract in which he promised that, if the goddesss fulfilled his wish, he would donate an altar. The *VSLM* formula is a standard one. The fire corps had a military structure. The members tended to be soldiers and policemen rather than plain firemen. That explains the title *beneficarius* (privileged soldier) of the donor of the the altar just mentioned.

The worship of Fortuna is also on record in a latrine in Pompeii. Clement of Alexandria (writing ca AD 190), in his *Proptrepticus* (*Exhortation to the Greeks*, 4.45.1) informs us about the general Roman practice:

> 'The Romans, who ascribed their greatest successes to Fortune, and regarded her as a very great deity, carried her statue to the privy, and erected it there, assigning to her a fitting temple.'

To the left and right of the monumental eastern entrance of the Barracks black-and-white mosaics indicate the location of two bars and one small bar respectively, situated against the walls (now hardly visible). The most southern one features a (now hardly visible) Greek inscription in a frame with handles (*tabula ansata*), facing east (*CIL* S 4755b):

ΠΡΟΚΛΟC	*Proklos*
ΕΠΟΙΗCΕΝ	*made (the mosaic)*
(transcription: Proklos epoiēsen)	

The adjacent mosaic depicts a volute *crater*, facing north, and features a Latin inscription, facing east (*CIL* XIV S 4755a):

[PR]OCLUS	*Proklos*
FECIT	*has made (the mosaic),*
M(iles) C(ohortis) S(ua) I(mpensa)	*soldier of the cohort, at his own expense*

The northern mosaic shows only a chalice *crater* in a double frame, facing south. Craters were used to mix wine with water (see no 4). The inscriptions and craters are oriented in such a way that they can be read and seen most easily by firemen entering or leaving the main gate.

The mosaics are dated to the first half of the 3rd century AD. Proclus is more likely to be the name of the soldier than of the mosaicist, since it is unlikely that the name of the giver would not be mentioned. In addition, *epoièsen* and *fecit* mean 'he made' or 'he had it made'. Proclus is a *cognomen* (surname) of Greek origin. The soldier may have migrated from a Greek-speaking region to Rome. If he was not from outside Italy, the Greek inscription was intended for Greek-speaking consumers. Proclus was the owner or tenant of the bars, which were primarily aimed at the inhabitants of the Barracks. C. Pavolini discounts the interpretation of MC as *miles cohortis* as no cohort number is mentioned. If he is right, Proclus was not a soldier but a concessionaire.

6. THE THEATRE (II, vii, 2)

A very fragmentary inscription (not in situ; *CIL* XIV 82) bearing the name of consul Marcus Vipsanius Agrippa ([*M(arcus) Ag]rippa co(n)s(ul)* [---] *po*[*testate*---]), which was found in the seating area (*cavea*) of the theatre, proves that the theatre was built by the son-in-law and powerful general of the emperor Augustus, probably just before 17 BC, as he received his *tribunicia potestas* in 18 BC. He died in 12 BC. He was responsible for the creation of countless buildings throughout the empire, among which the predecessor of the Hadrianic Pantheon in Rome.

Attached to the back wall, perhaps not in its original place, is a greatly restored dedicatory inscription. It reads (*CIL* XIV 114):

IMP(erator) CAES(ar) DIVI M(arci) ANTONINI FILIUS
DIVI COMMODI FRATER DIVI ANTONINI PII
NEPOS DIVI HADRIANI PRONEPOS DIVI TRAIANI
PARTHICI ABNEPOS DIVI NERVAE ADNEPOS
L(ucius) SEPTIMIUS SEVERUS PIUS PERTINAX AUG(ustus)
ARABICUS ADIABENICUS P(ater) P(atriae) PONTIF(ex) MAX(imus)
TRIBUNIC(ia) POTEST(ate) IIII IMP(erator) {VI}II CO(n)S(ul) II ET
MARCUS AURELIUS ANTONINUS CAESAR
 DEDICAVERUNT

Imperator Caesar, son of the divine Marcus Antoninus (Pius), brother of the divine Commodus, grandson of the divine Antoninus Pius, great-grandson of the divine Hadrianus, great-great-grandson of the divine Trajanus Parthicus, great-great-great-grandson of the divine Nerva, Lucius Septimius Severus Pius Pertinax Augustus, Arabicus Adiabenicus, father of the fatherland, highest priest, endowed with the power of tribune of the people for the fourth time, imperator for the second time (II should be read instead of the incorrectly reconstructed VIII), *consul for the second time, and Marcus Aurelius Antoninus Caesar have dedicated*

The inscription was made during or after the enlargement of the theatre in AD 198. This implies that the facelift can be dated to around that year. The emperor was very popular in Ostia. He probably enlarged the Grandi Horrea (the Great Granary, on the north side of the *decumanus*), restored the Piccolo Mercato (Little Market, near the Capitolium), and may have constructed a semicircular harbour (*emporium*) not far from the mouth of the Tiber. When he died, there was enough grain for seven years. Bronze medallions testify to the interest in the grain supply of his predecessor and brother Commodus who, after a food crisis in AD 189, created the African grain fleet, in addition to the already existing Alexandrian one. These fleets were protected by war galleys.

Originally the theatre could hold 3000 spectators. After the rebuilding its capacity increased to 4000. The building consisted of the *cavea* (the sitting area), the *orchestra* (the central open space), the *frons scaenae* (a façade with niches) and a *pulpitum* (podium) on which plays were enacted. Persons with a high social rank sat on the front, lowest seats, above them sat members of the middle class, and the upper part was reserved for women and slaves.

In accordance with the directions of Vitruvius' *De architectura*, a book dedicated to the emperor Augustus, the *cavea* was not oriented to the south in order to avoid the sun blinding visitors and temperatures becoming too high. Originally the rear wall of the *frons* had the same height as the highest gallery wall of the *cavea*. Its décor was a façade decorated with columns, gates and niches with statues. Nowadays only marble Medusa masks remain. Under the *cavea*, alongside the *decumanus*, were shops where spectators could buy refreshments during an interval. Only the most important spectators could enter the theatre through a central corridor between the shops. Equally in line with Vitruvius' directions is a peristyle, a garden-like space with porticoes (*porticus post scaenam*), behind the theatre, now called Square of the Guilds (Piazzale delle Corporazioni).

Around AD 400 the theatre was adapted so that the *orchestra* could be filled with water. Two shops were transformed into water cisterns. Besides tragedies and comedies water spectacles could be arranged, for example choreographic performances with amorous intrigues between sea gods and goddesses. The actors may have been naked, thereby attracting a large public.

In late antiquity the entrance corridor was filled with statue bases from the Square of the Guilds, probably when Ragonius Vincentius Celsus, *praefectus annonae* from AD 385 to August 389, restored the theatre. He reused one statue base from the Square, now standing to the southeast of the theatre, near the *decumanus* (*CIL* XIV S 4716; see below, no 7, base no 4; *fig. 11*):

RAGONIUS VINCENTIUS
CELSUS V(ir) C(larissimus) PRAEFECTUS
ANNONAE URBIS ROMAE
URBI EIDEM PROPRIA
PECUNIA CIVITATIS
OSTIENSIUM COLLOCAVIT

Ragonius Vincentius Celsus, a very renowned man, prefect of the grain supply of the city of Rome, placed (a statue) for the same city with the own money of the city of the Ostienses

This Christian magistrate organized restoration activities in Ostia and in Portus (see nos 18 and 20). Therefore he was elected as *patronus perpetuus*

Fig. 11. Statue base in front of the Theatre (photo author).

('patron for life') of both cities. Though he was Christian, he probably placed a statue of the personification of Roma on the base.

Behind the theatre stands a small marble altar, dated to the 2nd century AD. The inscription reads (*CIL* S 4319):

NUMINI
DOMUS
AUGUSTI
VICTOR ET
HEDISTUS
VERN(ae) DISP(ensatores)
   CUM
TRAIANO
AUG(usti) LIB(erto)
A $\overline{\text{X}}$ M̊ (= a decem milibus modiorum)

To the Divine Power of the Imperial House. Victor and Hedistus, houseborn slaves (and) pay clerks together with Traianus, freedman of the Emperor who granted financial privileges to builders of ships of 10,000 modii.

R. Meiggs suggests that due to a decree of the emperor Claudius the freedman Traianus was responsible for compensations to be given to builders of ships with a load of no less than 10,000 *modii* (70 tons) who worked in the service of the *annona* (grain supply). Suetonius (*Life of Claudius* 18) writes:

> 'He (Claudius) proposed to the merchants a sure profit, by indemnifying them against any loss that might befall them by storms at sea; and granted great privileges to those who built ships for that traffic.'

The number of 10,000 *modii* is mentioned by Gaius, *Inst.* 1.32 and Ulpian, *Reg.* 3.6.

A modius is a measure containing ca 9 litres of grain. Victor and Hedistus (from Greek *Hedistos*) were *vernae*, house-born slaves, in this case born in the imperial house. They may have paid other persons who were involved in the grain supply.

The left side of the altar features an erased wine pitcher, the right side a *patera* (dish).

The altar may have belonged to the Temple on the Square if the latter was indeed dedicated to the emperor cult (see below).

7. THE SQUARE OF THE GUILDS (PIAZZALE DELLE CORPORAZIONI; II, vii, 4)

Behind the theatre three porticoes give access to sixty-one adjacent small rooms, used as commercial offices. The corridor in front of the stalls is paved with black-and-white mosaics, often including texts which record the proprietors and their place of origin. What most mosaics have in common, is their overseas trade relation with Roman cities in the Mediterranean, in North Africa, Alexandria, Sardinia and Gallia. Captains, shippers and merchants could make business contacts there with representatives from their home city who held residence in Ostia. Some scholars presume that the latter sponsored performances in the theatre. Most mosaics are dated after ca AD 140, more precisely to ca 190-200. It is not impossible that many shippers belonged to Commodus' African grain fleet, mentioned before.

Only the first two mosaics, in the eastern portico, mention guilds (*corpora*) so that the modern name of the square is incorrect. The last mosaics (close to the theatre) in the western *porticus* (nos 51-52, 56-57) have non-commercial themes like hunting, are on a lower level and can be dated between ca 50 and 140 (*CIL* XIV S 4549). Only mosaics with legible texts are dealt with here. Several are framed by a *tabula ansata*, a table with two handles, like the sign of a building (see no 19). One marble tympanum with an inscription reading *naviculari africani* (African shippers), found in the east portico, proves that the offices were roofed.

1.
[C]LODIUS PRIMIGENIUS
[CL]AUDIUS CRESCENS Q(uin)Q(uennales)
STUPPATORES RES[TIONES]

Clodius Primigenius (and) Claudius Crescens, guild presidents for five years. Makers of and traders in hemp, and rope-makers (fig. 12).

Ropes were indispensable for ships and for this reason the guild had an office next to many shipmasters from elsewhere. The workshop, headquarters and temple of the rope-makers is just to the west of the Round Temple (I, x, 3-4), near the Forum. The workers made ropes from flax, espartograss (alphagrass with short and thin fibres) and hemp. *Stuppa* is a Greek loan word, meaning tow or flax. The process was as follows. The flax was dried on land. Then it was placed in warm water in the workshop, and dried in

Fig. 12. Mosaic in the Square of the Guilds (photo author).

a closed corridor next to the workshop or on its roof. When it was dry, the flax was struck with a wooden hammer or a block of stone, or grated over the sharp edge of a block to rid it of its fibres. Then it was combed in order to clean it. Ropes were made of this worked material. The guild temple was later converted to a *Mithraeum*, a sacred space for Mithras (see nos 22 and 44).

The guild presidents looked after the mosaic. The name Clodius is a plebeian form of the first name Claudius. An older mosaic, no 58, mentions only S. R., which means *stuppatores* (and) *restiones*.

2.
CORPUS PEL   *The guild of the furriers*
LION(um) OST(iensium) E(t) POR   *of Ostia and of Portus*
TE(nsium) HIC   *here*

3.
NAVICULARIORUM LIGNARIORUM   *[Office] of the shipmas-*
                                    ters who trade in wood

The mosaic shows a lighthouse flanked by ships. Wood was needed for several purposes, including house and ship building and the heating of the many baths in the city.

10.
NAVICULARI MISUENSES HIC   *The shipmasters of Misua here*

The mosaic shows two ships, and a tower flanked by fish. Misua (modern Sidi Daud in Tunisia) was a city in the proconsular *provincia* Africa.

11.
NAVICULARI MUILV[...]HIC   *The shipmasters from (?) Muilv... here*
MUS[LU[VI]A[NI]   *(shipmasters?) from Musluvium*

Musluvium (modern Sidi Rekane) was a place in Mauretania Sitifensis, in North Africa. The mosaic shows a little Amor on a dolphin, two other dolphins and two female heads in a medallion (seasons?).

12.
NAVICULAR[I H(ippone)] DIARRY(to)   *The shipmasters of Iulia*
                                    Hippo Diarrhytus

Iulia Hippo Diarrhytus (modern Bizerta in Tunisia) was a city in North Africa. Only a dolphin is visible.

14.
STAT(io) SABRATENSIUM   *The office of the Sabratenses*

Sabratha (modern Sabrata in Libya) also lies in North Africa. The elephant on the mosaic refers to the trade in wild animals and possibly in ivory.

15 and 16.
NAVICULAR(i) ET NEGOTIAN(tes) DE SUO

The shipmasters and traders at their own expense

17.
NAVICULARI GUMMITANI DE SUO

The shipmasters of Gummi at their own expense (fig. 13)

The city name Gummi (modern Bordj Cedria) occurs twice in North Africa, once in Byzacena and once near Carthago. At the centre of the mosaic a *modius* is visible, flanked by bent trees. A modius is a vessel that could contain 9 litres (6.5 kg) of grain.

Fig. 13. Mosaic in the Square of the Guilds (photo author).

18.
NAVICU(lar)I KARTHAG(inienses) DE SUO

The shipmasters of Carthage at their own expense

Carthago is located on the spot of modern Tunis.

19.
NAVIC(ulari) TURRITANI   *The shipmasters of Turris*

There were several cities with this name. Here it is Turris Libisonis (modern Porta Torres) on Sardinia, as the following mosaic no 21 also mentions a Sardinian city. Both were involved in the grain supply.

21.
NAVICUL(ari) ET NEGOTIANTES   *The shipmasters and traders*
      KARALITANI   *of Karales*

The *modius* refers to the grain that was transported from Karales (modern Cagliari) on Sardinia.

23.
N(avicvlariis) F(eliciter)   *Good luck to the shipmasters*
[NAVIC]ULARI SYLLECTI[NI]   *The shipmasters of Syllectum*
NE(gotiantes)   *merchants*

Syllectum was a city in North Africa (Tunisia). The shipmasters probably transported oil. The mosaic depicts two boats, a lighthouse, and two dolphins attacking a squid.

24.
N(aviculariis) F(eliciter)   *Good luck to the shipmasters*

32.
[NAVI(culari)] NARBONENSES   *The shipmasters of Narbo*

Narbo Martius (modern Narbonne) was a city in Gallia. The building to the right of the ship is a lighthouse.

34.
NAVICULARI CURBITANI D(e) S(uo)
S(tatio) N(egotiatorum) F(rumentariorum) C(oloniae) C(urbitanae)

The shipmasters of Curubis at their own expense.
The office of grain traders of the colonia Curubis.

The Colonia Iulia Curubis (modern Kourba in Tunisia) was a city in North Africa. Two dolphins flank a lighthouse (compare statio no 17)

38.
S(tatio) F(rumentariorum) C(orporis)
S(tatio) F(eliciter) C(orporis)

The office of the guild of the grain traders.
The office of the guild. Good luck.

A *modius* is present between dolphins.

40.
[ALE]XANDRIA   *Alexandria*

This office was owned by the shipmasters from Alexandria in Egypt. There is no indication of the nature of transported goods. Most of the grain came from Egypt.

43.
CODICARI DE SUO   *The Tiber-shippers at their own expense*

48.
M(auretania) C(aesariensis)

The initials of the *provincia* Mauretania Caesariensis in North Africa (Tunesia and the western part of Algeria) are visible on the amphora. The vase refers to the wine trade in the Severan period, from AD 193 onwards. The flanking palm trees refer to commerce in dates.

58.
S(tuppatores) R(estiones) *Makers of/traders in hemp, (and) rope-makers*

The mosaic dates to the first half of the 1st century AD because it is on a lower level. It depicts plants and instruments for rope-making.

7.1. The statue bases in the garden of the Square of the Guilds

The Square has many statue bases for men who among other things had promoted the well-being of the city, especially the grain trade, in the 2nd and 3rd centuries AD. Some statues of *togati* have been preserved. The inscription on the pedestal in front of office 48 (west side) reads (*fig. 14*):

P(ublio) NONIO P(ublii) FIL(io)
PAL(atina) LIVIO
ANTEROTIANO
EQUO PUBL(ico) EXORNATO AB
IMP(eratore) M(arco) AURELIO ANTONINO AUG(vsto)
DEC(reto) DEC(urionum) DECUR(ioni) ADLECTO
FLAMINI DIVI HADRIANI
SALIO LAURENT(ivm) LAVINATIUM
AEDILI PR(aetori) SACR(is) VOLK(ani) FACIU(ndis)
T(itus) TINUCIUS
SOSIPHANES
  CARISSIMO
  PIENTISSIMO
L(ocus) D(atus) D(ecreto) D(ecurionum) P(ublice)

For Publius Nonius Livius Anterotianus from (the tribus*) Palatina, son of Publius, honoured by the Emperor Marcus Aurelius Antoninus Augustus with a horse at public expense, appointed as town councillor by decree of the town council, priest of the divine Hadrian, Salian priest of the inhabitants of Laurentum and Lavinium, aedile, praetor for making sacred things of (for) Volkanus (Vulcanus). Titus Tinucius Sosiphanes (erected this statue) for his very beloved and faithful friend. The place is given by a decision of the town councillors, at public expense*

Publius Nonius Livius Anterotianus was *eques Romanus* (member of the *ordo equester*) and *decurio* (member of the town council), probably between AD 161 and 180. The tribal indication Palatina shows his Ostian origin. A tribus was a subdivision of the Roman citizen body.

    Ostia had at least three important places for statues: this square, the Forum and the Campus of Magna Mater (Cybele). The Square forms an

Fig. 14. Statue base in Square of the Guilds (photo author).

architectural unity with the theatre. The covered colonnade around the square was used to protect the spectators against rain, just as Vitruvius prescribed. In the time of the emperor Claudius the level was raised. The temple in the centre, dated by means of brick stamps to just before AD 96, was built under the emperor Domitian. It is not completely sure to which deity it was dedicated. Vulcanus, Ceres and Pater Tiberinus (Father Tiber) have been suggested, but none with cogent arguments. Recent research suggests that it was destined for the emperor cult. The level of the square was raised again under Hadrian. The temple may have received its lateral annexes between 140 and 172 (*CIL* XIV 246: *ordo corporator(um) qui pecuniam ad ampliand(um) templum contuler(unt)* (The association of (200!) guild members that brought money together in order to expand the temple).

For the sake of completeness here follows, in alphabetical order, the list of the names of the honorands mentioned in the inscriptions of all sixteen statue bases in alphabetical order of family names (*nomina gentilicia*), their *CIL*- or *AE*-number, date, find spot, present position, and dedicants:

1. Q. Acilius Fuscus = *CIL* XIV 154; date: 198-211; Theatre. North part of the Square. Dedicants: *corpus me(n)sorum frument(ariorum) adiutorum et acceptorum ost(iensium)* (the guild of the grain measurers, assistants and receivers of Ostia).
2. Q. Aeronius Antiochus = *CIL* XIV S 4140; date: end of the 2nd century; Theatre. East part of the Square. Dedicant: *Aninia Anthis coniunx* (wife).
3. P. Aufidius Fortis = *CIL* XIV S 4620; date: 146; Square, southeast part, near the temple; found in situ. Dedicants: *corpus mercatorum frumentariorum* (the guild of the grain merchants).
4. P. Aufidius Fortis = *CIL* XIV S 4621; *AE* 1910, 195; date: ca 146; found to the southeast of the theatre, but originating from the the Theatre and ultimately from the Square. Dedicants: *(Fa)ustinianus, Epictetus, Frosynus, Ianuarius*. The base was reused by Ragonius Vincentius Celsus (385-389). He is mentioned on the back of the base (*CIL* XIV S 4716), now facing the theatre.
5. Q. Calpurnius Modestus = *CIL* XIV S 161; date: ca 161-180; Theatre. North part of the Square, near the temple. Dedicants: *corpus mercatorum frumentariorum* (guild of the grain merchants).
6. P. Flavius Priscus = *CIL* XIV 4452; *AE* 1913, 189; date: 1 March 249; Square: southeast part, near the temple; found in situ. Dedicants: *corpus me(n)sorum frum(entariorum) ost(iensium)* (the guild of the Ostian grain measurers). The same Flavius is mentioned on the reused base in the Hercules temple (no 21).
7. C. Iulius Tyrannus = *CIL* XIV 370; date: 165-169; Theatre. Northeast part of the Square. Dedicants: *universi honorati (of the collegium fabr(um) tignuar(iorum) ostis)* (all honorary members of the guild of the builders at Ostia).
8. M. Iunius Faustus = *CIL* XIV S 4142; date: 173; Theatre. Northeast corner of the Square. Dedicants: *domini navium Afrarum universarum item Sardorum* (the owners of all the African ships and of the Sardinians).
9. M. Licinius Privatus = *CIL* XIV 374; date: ca 200; Theatre. Directly behind the temple. Dedicants: *universus numerus caligatorum collegi fabrum tignuariorum osti(en)s(ium)* (the whole number of booted members of the guild of the Ostian builders).
10. P. Non(ius) L(ivius) Anterotianus = *CIL* XIV 390; date: 161-180; Theatre. Northwest corner of the Square. Dedicant: *Livia Marcellina*.
11. P. Nonius Livius Anterotianus = *CIL* XIV 391; date: 161-180; Theatre. West side of the square. Dedicant: *T. Tinucius Sosiphanes*. See p. 37 for a translation.
12. Q. Petronius Melior = *CIL* XIV 172; date: 3 February 184; Theatre.

West side of the square. Dedicants: *corpus me(n)sorum frum(entariorum) ost(iensium)* (the guild of the Ostian grain measurers).
13. Sex. Publicius Maior = *CIL* XIV S 4143 (fragment); date: probably 161-180; Theatre. Now in one of the northwest stationes. Dedicants: unknown.
14. ... Rubrius ... = *CIL* XIV S 4664; *AE* 1913, 190; date: probably end of the 2nd century; Square. Southwest corner of the Square. Dedicant: *T. Rubrius Eupator* (son of a Rubrius).
15. P. Veturius Testius Amandus = *CIL* XIV S 4144; date: 147; Theatre. To the west of the temple. Dedicants: *universi navigiarii corpor(a) quinque* (i.e.: *lenuncularior(um) ostiens(ium)*) (all shippers, five guilds (of the Ostian tug-boat shippers)).
16. Inscription on a side of the base = *CIL* XIV S 4148; date: 30 December 166. Under the inscription is a vertical stem in relief. Theatre. Northwest of the temple. The inscription on the front has been erased. Dedicants: unknown.

The dates, based on the number of *lustra* (five-year periods) of guilds or on the imperial and consular names mentioned in the inscriptions, cover AD 146, 147, 150, 166, 166/7, 173, 161-180, 184, 198-211 and 249. The bases with a 'probable date' belong to the 2nd century in view of their form, the frame of the inscriptions, the layout of the text and the typeface.

No base can be dated before ca 146. This may be explained by the fact that during Hadrian's reign the square level was raised, and the back entrance on the Tiber side was closed. Now the question arises whether the inscriptions shed light on the function of the temple and the square. In nine cases *collegia* or *corpora* are involved, not only guilds related to the grain trade but also guilds of the *fabri tignuari* (builders) and the *lenuncularii* (river boatmen, bargemen). Therefore, there is no reason to suggest that the temple was dedicated to Ceres.

It is interesting to note that five of the fourteen known dedicants are not guilds but private persons. This implies that the square was not only a place 'peculiarly associated with the guilds' as was suggested by Meiggs. Interestingly, the honorands in the five private dedications are, *inter alia*, priest, *sevir aug(ustalis)* (list no 2), *flamen* of a deified emperor, Titus (list no 8), Vespasian (list no 14), and Hadrian (list nos 10 and 11). Nonius (list nos 10-11) and Rubrius (list no 14) were also *decuriones adlecti* (co-opted town councillors) but not members of *corpora* (guilds). Iunius (list no 8) was successively *decurio adlectus, flamen divi Titi, mercator frumentarius, quaestor aerarii, flamen Romae et Augusti, patronus corporis curatorum navium marinarum*. This shows that a *flamen Titi* was not automatically *flamen Romae et Augusti* and that as a consequence he was successively related to two temples of *divi*. He is honoured by the *domini navium Afrarum universarum*, the anonymous owners of all African ships, not known as a guild.

The inscriptions do not prove that the square temple was dedicated to deified emperors, but the striking correspondence between private dedicants and the function of *flamen divi* (priest of a deified emperor) of four honorands supports rather than disproves my interpretation. There is, however, another strong indication.

The inscription on a monumental tomb near Porta Romana (see no 42a) informs us that the town council honoured C. Domitius Fabius Hermogenes with a public funeral and an equestrian statue on the Forum (see no 16): he was *flamen* of the deified Hadrianus, ...*in cuius sacerdotio solus ac primus lud[os] [scaenic]os sua p[e]cunia fecit*... (...during his priesthood he was the just and only person who sponsored theatrical performances at his own expense...). This implies that sponsoring of theatre plays took place after AD 139, probably for the first time around AD 200. Since it was in his capacity of *flamen divi Hadriani* that he took the initiative to sponsor games, it appears likely that he was connected with the temple behind the Theatre.

Nine bases were placed by decree of the *decuriones*. The abbreviation *L.D.D.D.*, *locus datus decurionum decreto* (the place (was) given by decree of the city councillors), is not mentioned by the inscriptions of base list no 1 (Acilius, *procurator annonae*, who had also held several functions outside Ostia), nos 3 and 4 (Aufidius, *IIvir, quaestor aerarii ostiensium*), no 6 (Flavius, *equestris ordinis*), and no 12 (Petronius, *procurator annonae*), perhaps because no permission was needed in view of their high status.

The bases with their statues were intended to commemorate men with special merit. They are also interesting for ritual reasons. On the occasion of the dedication of a statue, *sportulae* (baskets with food) were distributed and *ludi* (games), obviously in the Theatre, were sponsored. This 'euergetic' behaviour shows the link between honorands and the Theatre. It supports D. Steuernagel's suggestion that proprietors of *stationes* (offices) may have sponsored theatre plays.

In conclusion it seems likely that from the end of the 1st century onwards the temple in the garden must have served gods who were of common interest: deified emperors. The last deified emperor mentioned in Ostian inscriptions (found so far) is Septimius Severus. After his reign, the emperor cult was possibly transferred to the Round Temple, built between ca 225 and 250 in the centre of the city, to the west of the Forum.

Most bases were reused as *spolia* in the central corridor of the Theatre around AD 400. After the excavation most of them were placed back on the Square.

Four statue bases, now in the Square, in front of and behind the temple, do not bear inscriptions or decorations. Some exhibit remains of a frame. So apparently inscriptions were made on the spot.

8. The Shrine of the Altar of the Twins
(Sacello dell'Ara dei Gemelli; II, vii, 3)

In the southwest of the Square of the Guilds there is a sacred room with benches, probably dating to the second half of the 2nd century AD. In the centre stands a plaster copy of a marble altar, converted into a statue base (*fig. 15*). The original is in the Museo Nazionale Romano, in Palazzo Massimo alle Terme, in Rome (*fig. 16*).

Apart from abundant reliefs which will be dealt with shortly, there are inscriptions (*CIL* XIV 51).

On the west side, the original front of the altar, above Mars and Venus in the relief we find:

P(ublius) AELIUS TROPHIMI AUG(usti) L(iberti) PROC(uratoris) PROV(inciae)
CRETAE LIB(ertus) SYNEROS ET
TROPHIMUS ET AELIANUS FILI

Publius Aelius Syneros, freedman of (P. Aelius) Trophimus, (who was in his turn) freedman of the emperor (and) procurator of the provincia *Creta and his sons Trophimus and Aelianus*

On the west side cornice:

[A]RAM SAC[RAM] [AD ANN?]ONAM
AUG(usti) GENIO [---]
SACOMAR[II]

Sacred altar (obj.) near (the statue of) Annona (Grain supply)
to the Genius of the Emperor [---]
the public weighers (subj.) [---](have dedicated)

Fig. 15. Altar/statue base in the Shrine of the Twins. Copy (photo author).

Fig. 16. Altar/statue base (Rome, Museo Nazionale Romano; photo author).

On the west side plinth:

DECURIONUM DECRETO *By decree of the town councillors*

On the south side plinth:

DEDICATA K(alendis) OCTOBR(is) M(anio)
ACILIO GLABRIONE C(aio) BELLICO TORQUATO CO(n)S(ulibvs)

Dedicated on 1 October when Manius Acilius Glabrio (and) Gaius Bellicus Torquatus were consuls (AD 124)

On the north side cornice (added when the altar was reused as statue base):

VOTUM SILVANO *Dedicated to Silvanus*

The altar was discovered during excavations in 1881. The inscription on the south side plinth provides the date 1 October AD 124, during the reign of Hadrian. It is based on the names of the two consuls who were in power in that year. The inscription on the west side cornice suggests that the shrine belonged to the guild of the *sacomarii* (public weighers). The word derives from the Greek word *sakoma* (counterpoise). They weighed grain with officially approved weighs.

First incense was burnt on the altar, followed by a libation of wine. The covering stone on the altar was fireproof and firmly consolidated with plugs. The sacrifices were probably intended for the war god Mars. This much can be inferred from the reliefs on the four sides.

The west side shows the loving couple Mars and Venus, with an Amor and a goose. The god of marriage, Hymenaeus, is also present which suggests that the two deities are married to each other.

On the north side little Amores are represented. They carry the armour of Mars. He did not need it during his meeting with Venus.

The east side features the personification of the Tiber as river god. His left hand rests upon a water vessel. To the left, in front of him, we see the twins Romulus and Remus, nurtured by a she-wolf and discovered by a few shepherds who are visible above the scene. Mars was the father of the twins.

The relief of the south side shows a number of little Amores around Mars' empty chariot.

The images refer to the divine ancestors of the Romans: Mars and Venus. Mars was the father of the city founders Romulus and Remus, while

Venus was the ancestral mother of the Julio-Claudian emperors.

The scenes on the south and north side are both oriented to the west. This suggests that the west side was the original front of the altar.

The room is of more recent date than the altar. This implies that the altar was transferred from another place. In a second instance it was dedicated to Silvanus, the old Italic god of the woods, judging from the inscription on the north side cornice. He was worshipped by farmers and, in addition, associated with *sacomarii*. So the relief featuring Romulus and Remus became the front, understandable since the curved staffs of the shepherds resemble the *pedum* of Silvanus. The altar became a base for the god's statue. It was consolidated with lead.

It is not known where the altar originally stood. The words *decurionum decreto* imply that it stood in a public place when it was dedicated in 124. Who transferred the base and when, is unknown. It may have happened when most offices were decorated with mosaics, around 200.

9. THE FOUR SMALL TEMPLES (QUATTRO TEMPIETTI; II, viii, 2)

Whoever passes the theatre sees to his right an open space with the remains of four small temples on a high podium. The temple on the far right has a little marble altar with an inscription, dated to around AD 150 (*CIL* XIV S 4127):

VENERI SACRUM   *Sacred to Venus*

A famous inscription from Portus (*CIL* XIV 375; Appendix 3) gives a possible clue as to who the deities of the other temples were. It mentions a powerful and rich man, Publius Lucilius Gamala, who at his own expense built temples for Venus, Fortuna, Ceres, goddess of agriculture and grain, and Spes, goddess of Hope, probably around 50 BC. The deities can be associated with the *annona*, the grain supply of Rome. The public domain (*ager publicus*) on which the temples were built was earmarked for storing grain.

Publius Lucilius was priest of Vulcanus and magistrate during the Republican Period, between ca 75 and 37 BC (see no 28). His surname Gamala may indicate that his ancestors came, around 80 BC, from the city of Gamala, to the east of the Lake of Galilea. His family was still powerful in the 2nd century AD. Large gifts, financing of buildings and restorations and the preservation of ancient cults run like a continuous thread through the family's history. A descendant of Lucilius Gamala who lived during the Antonine period financed the restoration of a temple of Venus, possibly this one (*CIL* XIV 376; Appendix 4). A great-great-grandson of Gamala 'senior' is mentioned in the inscription *AE* 1994, 254; 2004, 360. He defended the public cause in the Senate in Rome.

The left and right side of the Venus altar feature reliefs showing a wine pitcher and a patera (libation dish).

A covered up black-and-white mosaic in the westernmost temple (*CIL* XIV S 4134) mentions two *duoviri* (mayors): the famous C. Cartilius Poplicola (mayor for the fifth time; see also nos 21 and 29) and C. Fabius, who, together with five freedmen, was responsible for a building activity, probably a renovation, after 23 BC.

10. THE SANCTUARY OF JUPITER (SACELLO DI GIOVE; II, viii, 4)

The space in front of the four temples harbours a square, walled sanctuary on the right-hand side, roofless even in antiquity, with a small travertine stone with the following identical inscription in each corner: IOMS (*CIL* XIV S 4292; *fig. 17*), which means:

I(ovi) O(ptimo) M(aximo) S(acrum)

Fig. 17. Cippus dedicated to Jupiter Optimus Maximus (photo author).

The sacred room was dedicated to the supreme god Jupiter, the Best and the Greatest. There is some doubt as to whether S means *sacrum*. F. Coarelli suggests: Sarapis or Sabazios. The four inscriptions, however, are dated ca 40-30 BC, a period in which an assimilation of Iupiter with an eastern deity is improbable. The walls date to the 1st century AD. In the Hadrianic period a *nymphaeum*, or fountain, was built to the north.

11. THE PERTINAX INSCRIPTION AND THE GUILD TEMPLE OF THE BUILDERS (TEMPIO COLLEGIALE; V, xi, 1)

Along the north side of the *decumanus*, in front of the former area, there is a fragmentary inscription. It consists of two blocks of marble, now placed on the remains of a wall. The following text, damaged by a *damnatio memoriae* can be reconstructed as follows (*CIL* XIV S 4365; 4382; *AE* 1971, 64):

DIVO PIO [P]ERTINACI AU[G(usto)]
  COLLEG(ium) FABR(um) [TIGNUAR(iorum)] O[ST(iensium)] [[---]]
CURAM AGENTIBUS C(aio) PLOTIO CA[---] SALINATORE IANUARIO L(ucio) FAIANIO /
OLYMPO MAG(istris) Q̄(uin)Q̄(uennalibvs) LUST(ri) X[XVIII]

To divine Pius Pertinax Augustus the Guild of the Builders of Ostia [[---]] while Gaius Plotius Ca[---], Salinator Ianuarius (and) Lucius Faianius Olympus, guild presidents for five years of the twenty-eighth lustrum, oversaw it

The inscription has been found at the crossroads of the *decumanus* and the Street of the *Augustales*. It was part of the architrave of the façade of the nearby guild temple (Tempio Collegiale), on the other side of the *decumanus* (Reg. V, xi, 1). The construction of the temple commenced under the emperor Commodus, AD 180-192, but it was later dedicated to the deified emperor Pertinax, Septimius Severus' predecessor, who was murdered in AD 193. Septimius respected him and included the names Pius Pertinax Augustus in his own name (see no 6). The inscription, therefore, may be dated to or soon after AD 193. From the number of *lustra* (periods of five years) it can be deduced that the Guild was founded in AD 53. It had a splendid clubhouse (*schola*) with banquet rooms on the south side of the *decumanus*, not far from the Forum (see no 17). Its building activities may have been stimulated by the emperors mentioned.

12. The Boundary Stones of the Public Domain
(*Ager Publicus*; II, ix, 2)

Along the north side of the *decumanus*, in front of the Grandi Horrea (The Great Granary), there is a modern metal fence behind which lie two travertine boundary stones with inscriptions, more than one metre below street-level (next to Reg. II, ix, 1; *fig. 18*). The one on the right reads (*CIL* XIV S 4702d):

C(aius) CANINIUS C(ai) F(ilius)	*Gaius Caninius, son of Gaius,*
PR(aetor) URB(anus)	praetor urbanus, *by decree of*
DE SEN(atus) SENT(entia)	*the Senate (of Rome) has*
POPLIC(um) IOUDIC(avit)	*declared (this domain) public*

Along the north side of the *decumanus*, over a length of ca 600 m (ca 2000 Roman feet), stand six travertine boundary stones (four with identical texts). The first, small one stands near Porta Romana (see no 1), the fourth to the south of the Claudian Great Granary (II, ix). They have been preserved at their original level, ca 1 metre below the 2nd century AD street level. They are dated to the 2nd century BC. Suggestions vary from ca 140 to 80 BC. No Gaius Caninius, praetor of Rome, is known from this period.

Fig. 18. Boundary stones along the decumanus *(photo author).*

However, he must have been active before Ostia became a *colonia*, probably around 63 BC. The Gracchi (137-123 BC) distributed grain to the *plebs* of Rome. After 123 BC, some 320.000 people received it. In that period the area between the *decumanus* and the Tiber may have been earmarked for storing grain. Few remains of early stores have been found. In that time the Tiber ran along and almost parallel to the *ager publicus* (public domain). Its left bank may have functioned as a not easily accessible river harbour for sea ships. In the 1st and 2nd centuries AD many buildings were built in the public space, but they were not all public in character as is sometimes suggested.

The most western stone of Caninius, mentioned above, is flanked on the left by a smaller boundary stone, also of travertine, bearing the following inscription (*CIL* XIX S 4703):

[P]RIVATUM (the characters UM are combined in a ligature)
AD TIBERIM
USQUE AD   *Private (domain) to the Tiber, up to the*
AQUAM   *water*

Thus the area to the west of the *ager publicus* was private.

The words 'up to the water' probably refer to the use of the riverbank, not to the building upon it, because riverbanks were the property of Rome. This may be deduced from inscriptions on a travertine boundary stone, which now stands in front of the local museum (*CIL* XIV S 4704):

C(aius) ANTISTIUS C(ai) F(ilius) C(ai) N(epos) VETUS
C(aius) VALERIUS L(uci) F(ilius) FLACC(us) TANUR(ianus)
P(ublius) VERGILIUS M(arci) F(ilius) PONTIAN(us)
P(ublius) CATENIUS P(ubli) F(ilius) SABINUS
TI(berius) VERGILIUS TI(beri) F(ilius) RUFUS
CURATORES RIPARUM ET ALVEI
TIBERIS EX S(enatu) C(onsulto) TERMINAVER(unt)
R(ecto) R(igore) L(ongum) P(edes) […]

Gaius Antistius Vetus, son of Gaius, grandson of Gaius, Gaius Valerius Flaccus Tanurianus, son of Lucius, Publius Vergilius Pontianus, son of Marcus, Publius Catenius Sabinus, son of Publius, Tiberius Vergilius Rufus, son of Tiberius, overseers of the banks and the bed of the Tiber, have drawn, by decree of the Senate, a borderline in a straight line for a length of […] feet

The text on the back of the stone reads:

SINE PRAEIUDICI[O]	*Without preceding public*
PUBLICO AUT	*decision or (decision) of*
PRIVATORUM	*private persons*

Five travertine stones bearing these texts have been found on the northern bank of the Tiber. The word public refers to the local authority of Ostia. Antistius was consul in AD 23; therefore the inscriptions may be dated to around that year. For a similar text on a square, travertine boundary stone from Rome, dated to 55/54 BC, see *CIL* VI 31540 h.

13. THE SMALL BASE FOR NEPTUNE, CASTOR AND POLLUX (I, xii, 3)

At the crossroads of the *decumanus* and the Semita dei Cippi, in the southwest corner, there is a small statue base with an inscription (*AE* 1955, 254) of which the original context is unknown:

NEPTUNO	*To Neptunus*
CASTORI	*Castor*
POLLUCI	*Pollux*
L(ucius) CATIUS	*Lucius Catius*
CELER	*Celer*
PR(aetor) URB(anus)	praetor urbanus
	(has dedicated it)

Not only Neptunus, the god of the sea, but also Castor and Pollux, who were twins and sons of Jupiter, were protectors of the seamen. It is unknown where the small base originally stood. The *praetor urbanus* of Rome came to Ostia every year, on 27 January, in order to celebrate the games - probably horse races - in honour of the twins (*ludi Castorum*). These took place in Isola Sacra, the area between Ostia and Portus, Ostia's two artificial harbours. A namesake of Catius, Publius Catius Sabinus, city prefect and consul for the second time in AD 216, had his visit commemorated in a work of art (see below). The small base may have been given by his son or grandson, who was consul between AD 239 and 242. In late antiquity the *praefectus urbi* or consul presided over the games. In a splendidly luxurious, large house, which now goes by the modern name 'House of the Dioscuri' (*Domus dei Dioscuri*; III, ix, 1), near *Porta Marina*, the twins are represented without horses in a polychrome mosaic dated to the second half of the 4th century. In that century the pagan games were still taking place, and they probably continued to do so until AD 394 when the emperor Theodosius closed pagan temples and forbade pagan activities.

An inscription on a lost marble base contains a poem in hexameters in which Catius Sabinus, evidently in his capacity of *praetor urbanus* of Rome, claims to have placed the work of art just mentioned (*CIL* XIV 1):

LITORIBUS VESTRIS QUONIAM CERTAMIN(a) LAETUM
EX(h)IBUISSE IUVAT CASTOR VENERANDEQUE POLLUX
MUNERE PRO TANTO FACIEM CERTAMINIS IPSAM
MAGNA IOVIS PROLES VESTRA PRO SEDE LOCAVI
URBA(n)IS CATIUS GAUDENS ME FASCIBUS AUCTUM
NEPTUNOQUE PATRI LUDOS FECISSE SABINUS

I Catius Sabinus, because I am glad that I was honoured with more urban fasces (symbols of power) and that I had organized games for father Neptunus, have placed the image of the game itself in front of your seat (temple) as it pleased me, o Castor and honourable Pollux, great sons of Jupiter, to have organized games on your coast in compensation for such a great duty (his being praetor urbanus*)*

The image was of course more of a relief than a painting. Recent research by M. Heinzelmann suggests that the temple stood on a large platform next to the Navalia (ship- or dockyard), on the left bank of the Tiber mouth. The temple faced the sea. It may date to the reign of Tiberius or Claudius. P. Lucilius Gamala who lived in the Antonine period restored the temple and the Navalia, once built by an unknown architect, Lucius Coilus: ... *aedem Castoris et Pollucis rest(ituit) ... navale a L. Coilio aedificatum extrue[n]tibus(?) fere collapsum restituit...* (*CIL* XIV 376; see Appendix 4).

The late classical author Ammianus records that, when in AD 359 storms prevented the grain ships from entering the harbour of Portus, the urban prefect Tertullus made a sacrifice in the temple of the Castores. It was successful, for the storm abated.

14. THE SANCTUARY OF THE LARES VICINALES
(PIAZZETTA DEI LARI; I, ii, 1)

In a rectangular, open space in the city quarter to the east of the Capitolium lie the remains of a rectangular building and a damaged, round, marble altar with an inscription, dated by P. Pensabene to ca 30-10 BC. The first two lines above the relief are visible as well as the third below it, on a raised level (*CIL* XIV S 4298; see cover photograph):

[M]AG(istri vici) D(e) S(ua) P(ecunia) F(aciendam) C(uraverunt)
   LARIBUS
     VICIN(alibus) SACR(am)

ARAM MARMOREAM

The officers of the neighbourhood had made at their own expense the sacred, marble altar for the Lares of the Neighbourhood

Magistri vici are known from Rome and elsewhere from the late-Republican period onwards. According to Suetonius (*Augustus* 30.2), Augustus divided Rome into regions and neighbourhoods (*vici*) and decreed that magistrates elected annually should look after the former and that officers (*magistri*) chosen from the people of each neighbourhood should look after the latter. This took place in 7 BC, when Rome was divided into 14 regions. In AD 73 there were 265 *vici*, also called *compita*, and by late antiquity there were more than 400, uneven subdivisions of regions. People of a neighbourhood worshipped the *Lares Augusti* in honour of the emperor. It was Augustus' intention to control the *plebs* and to foster social, political and religious cohesion.

As the altar inscription does not mention *Lares Augusti* or *Lares compitales*, it has to date to before 7 BC, which is in line with P. Pensabene's proposed date. In addition, no *vicus* is mentioned. Some have dated the altar to the Hadrianic period. The explicit referring to the fact that the altar is made of marble, however, suggests an early date too.

The reliefs depict a burning altar at the centre of the circular composition. It is approached from the left by Pan carrying a bucket and guiding a Lar, both dancing, by two dancing Lares, and from the right by a pig set to be sacrificed, by Hercules, wearing a lion skin, and by another Pan holding a bucket and guiding a Lar, both dancing. Behind the altar is a tree against which a *thyrsus*, the characteristic staff of Bacchus, god of wine, leans.

Both Hercules and Pan are illustrated in mythical, Bacchic processions, both could protect neighbourhoods, while Lares protected houses and city wards.

The altar may have been damaged by Christians.

Just to the east of the altar is a building from the Antonine period, which had three entrances. It possibly was a *compitum*, a sanctuary at the crossroads.

15. The Apartment building of Jupiter and Ganymedes (Caseggiato di Giove e Ganimede; I, iv, 2)

This high status corner building with an adjacent deep, inner garden, near the Capitolium, dated to the late Hadrianic period, is not accessible to the public. Some presume, incorrectly, that it was a kind of hotel, based on its erotic graffiti in bad Latin, dated to ca AD 200 (*CIL* XIV S 5291):

HIC AD CALLIN[I]CUM
FUTUI OREM ANUM AMICOM […]RE NOLITE R IN AEDI[…]

Here at Callinicus (in Callinicus' house) I have fucked in the mouth (and) the anus of a friend. Don't return to the house (?)

LIVIUS ME CUNNUS
LINCET TERTULLE CUNNU OV[---]
EFESIUS TERPSILLA AMAT

Livius (licks) my cunt, licks the cunt of Tertulla [---]; Efesius loves Terpsilla

AGATHOPUS ET PRIMA ET EPAPHRODITUS TRES CONVENIENTES

Agathopus and Prima and Epaphroditus (are) coming together as three (as a threesome)

The building's modern name is based on the impressive lost painting of Jupiter abducting the handsome boy Ganymedes, dated to ca AD 140. Jupiter fell in love with him and in the guise of an enormous eagle abducted him to the Olympus in order to make him his cup-bearer. Cunnilingus may also have been practised in the Baths of Trinacria (see no 25).

16. The Forum

The Forum, between the *decumanus* and the Temple of Roma and Augustus, opposite the Capitolium, was one of the places where statues were erected for eminent persons. Those on the Square of the Guilds (see no 7) were largely for magistrates who had been active in commerce. Those on the Forum were for those who had been engaged in politics.

In the south part of the forum some statue bases are still in their original location. The inscription on the base near the decumanus and the west corner of the Forum reads (*CIL* XIV S 4721; *fig. 19*):

TRANSLATAM EX SOR	*(Base) transferred from places,*
DENTIBUS LOCIS	*which are growing filthy, for the*
AD ORNATUM FORI	*decoration of the forum and for*
ET AD FACIEM PUBLICAM	*public display, under the care of*
CURANTE P(ublio) ATTIO	*Publius Attius Clementinus, a*
CLEMENTINO V(iro) C(larissimo)	*very renowned man, chief of the*
PRAEF(ecto) ANN(onae)	*grain supply*

On the left side the relief of an unfinished pitcher is visible and on the right side a sacrificial bowl. Parts of Ostia had already fallen into decay in the 3rd century AD. Some buildings, which had caught fire, were not even restored. Some small streets were closed. The inscription on the base can be dated to the end of the 4th century AD. A high official from Rome, chief of the grain supply, oversaw the transfer of the base.

A fragmentary statue base is visible in the southwest part of the Forum, in front of the temple of Roma and Augustus (*CIL* XIV S 4455):

*Fig. 19.
Statue base on the Forum
(photo author).*

MANILIO RU[STICO]
PRAEF(ecto) ANN(onae) A(genti) V(ices) PRA[E(fectorum) PRAETO-
RIO]
EEMM (= eminentissimorum) VV (= virorum) CURATO[RI ET P]A-
TRONO
SPLENDIDISSIM(a)E COL(oniae) OS[T(iensium)] OB EIUS FIDEM AC
MERi[T](a) ERGA REM PUBLICAM ORDO
ET POPULUS OSTIENSIUM [Q]UO CIVITAS
TITULIS ADMINISTRA[TI]ONIS EIUS
FIERET INLUSTR[IOR?] DECREVIT ADQ(ue)
      CONST[ITUI]T

For Manilius Rusticus, chief of the grain supply, deputizing for the chiefs of the emperor's bodyguard, very excellent men, curator and patron (protector) of the very splendid Colonia Ostiensis *because of his loyalty and merit to the city the town council and the people of the* Ostienses *decreed and set up (the base and statue) in order that the city community would be more famous as a result of the fame of his administration*

The socle originally supported an equestrian statue of Manilius Rusticus. The holes for the four horse legs are still visible on the top. The base is dated to the late 4th century AD. There are misspellings, for example adque instead of atque.

   Another statue base, on the east side, offers the following text (*CIL* XIV S 4717; *fig. 20*):

CURAVIT RAGONIU[S]
VINCENTIUS CELSUS
V(ir) C(larissimus) PRAEFECTUS
ANNONAE URBIS
ROMAE ET CIVITAS[IS]
FECIT MEMORATA
 DE PROPRIO

Ragonius Vincentius Celsus, a very renowned man, chief of the grain supply of the city of Rome oversaw it and the city (of Ostia) has made the things mentioned at its own expense

Ragonius Vincentius Celsus was chief of the grain supply between AD 385 and 389. Thanks to him the nearby Forum Baths underwent restora-

Fig. 20.
Statue base on the Forum (photo author).

tions (see no 18). Another, reused, statue base mentioning him stands in front of the Theatre (see no 7).

Several statues on the Forum must have been lost (see *Fasti Ostienses*, for the year AD 152). According to his epitaph, Gaius Domitius Hermogenes had a statue on the Forum (*CIL* XIV 353; see no 40).

17. THE GUILD-HOUSE OF THE BUILDERS
(CASEGGIATO DEI TRICLINI; I, xii, 1)

Directly east of the Forum lies the splendid clubhouse (*schola*) of the builders (*fabri tignuarii*: literally carpenters), dated to ca AD 120, in the Hadrianic period (see also no 11). The building has a central court. In the rear there is a chapel-like space with podia, used as a space for the worship of gods and deified emperors (see *CIL* S 4300). On the left side are four dining rooms with three stone benches (*triclinia*). In the left rear corner of the court there is a statue base which records 352 members of the guild on its left side (*fig. 21*). The inscription on the front, dedicated to Septimius Severus and dated to AD 198, reads (*AE* 1928, 123):

IN SITU INSCRIPTIONS

Fig. 21a-b. Statue base in the Guild-house of the Builders; a. left side; b. front (photos author)

IMP(eratori) CAESARI
DIVI MARCI ANTONINI
PII GERMAN(ici) SARMAT(ici) FIL(io)
DIVI COMMODI FRATRI

DIVI ANTONINI PII NEP(oti)
DIVI HADRIANI PRONEP(oti)
DIVI TRAIANI PART(hici) ABNEP(oti)
DIVI NERVAE ADNEP(oti)
L(ucio) SEPTIMIO SEVERO
PIO PERTINACI AUG(usto)
ARAB(ico) ADIAB(enico) PART(hico) MAX(imo) PONT(ifici) MAX(imo)
TRIB(unicia) POT(estate) VI IMP(eratori) XI CO(n)S(uli) II P(atriae) P(atriae) PROCO(n)S(uli)
NUMERUS CALIGATORUM
    DECUR(iarum) XVI

For Imperator Caesar,
son of the deified Marcus Antoninus
Pius Germanicus Sarmaticus,
brother of deified Commodus,
grandson of the deified Antoninus Pius
great-grandson of deified Hadrianus,
great-great-grandson of deified Traianus Parthicus
great-great-great-grandson of deified Nerva,
Lucius Septimius Severus
Pius Pertinax Augustus
Arabicus Adiabenicus Parthicus Maximus, high priest,
with tribunician power for the sixth time, imperator for the eleventh time,
consul for the second time, father of the fatherland, proconsul
the number of booted members
    of sixteen sections (have placed)

Evidently the quasi-military guild consisted of sixteen units comprising twenty-two men each. Chiefs of the *decuriae* (sections) were *decuriones*. The three presidents were *magistri quinquennales*, elected for a period of five years. The festivities, including dining and drinking, must have taken place on different occasions or at different times as the limited number of dining rooms could not hold 352 men.

18. The Forum Baths (Terme del Foro; I, xii, 6)

These public baths (*thermae Gavi Maximi*) to the south of the guild club are the largest of the town, built by Marcus Gavius Maximus, chief of the guard of the emperor Antoninus Pius, between ca AD 150 and 161 (*AE* 1971, 65). The building was restored in the 4th century. The floors and walls are richly decorated with marble slabs. Through a vestibule and entrance hall one arrives at the *apodyterium*, the undressing room. The octagonal space with large, open windows was used for sun bathing. From there one comes to the *sudatorium*, the room for sweating. Then follow two *tepidaria*, rooms with lukewarm water. The walls of the large second room feature many inscribed slabs which had been reused in the Baths. The second *tepidarium* gives access to the *caldarium*, the room with warm water in three basins.

In the northern part of the building are fragments of a marble architrave with a Greek inscription in a dactylic hexameter, a succession of one long and two short syllables. The original position of the architrave is not known. Judging by the content of the inscription it must have belonged to the building. The inscription reads (*SEG* 33, 773; *fig. 22*):

ΛΟΥΤΡΟΝ ΑΛΕΞΙΠΟ[ΝΟΝ] --- DE]ΙΞΕΝ
(transcription: loutron alexípo[non] --- [de]ixen)

A bath dispelling sorrow indicated (to build)

Fig. 22. Epistyle in the Forum Baths (photo author)

ΒΙΚΤΩΡ ΑΡΧΟC ΕΩΝ (not in situ) *Victor being chief*
(transcription: Biktōr archos eōn)

[…]ΚΥΔΙΜΟC ΑΥCΟΝΙΗC (*fig. 23*)
(transcription: […]kudimos Ausoniēs)

[…]famous of Italy (famous for his leadership in Italy)

The inscription refers to a restoration in the 4th century AD. If Biktor is Flavius Octavius Victor, a *praefectus annonae*, he repaired or embellished the baths after AD 331. That baths were believed 'to drive away care from the mind', may also be deduced from Augustine's *Confessiones* 9, 12, 32.

To the south of the building is the *palaestra*, the wrestling court. Here stands an unidentified temple, possibly belonging to a guild. Behind the temple are public toilets. Water from the baths could effectively be reused here. Under the baths runs a corridor which gives access to the furnace for the production of warm water. It is accessible via the *palaestra* along small stairs next to the building.

An inscription on a marble epistyle, preserved on an external wall on the southern side of the building, near the Forum, reads as follows (*CIL* XIV S 4718):

Fig. 23. Epistyle in the Forum Baths (photo author).

CURAVIT RAGONIUS VINCENTIUS CELSUS V(ir) C(larissimus) PRAEFECTUS ANNONAE URBIS ROMAE ET CIVITAS FECIT [MEMORATA DE PROPRIO]

Ragonius Vincentius Celsus, a very renowned man, chief of the grain supply of the city of Rome oversaw it and the city (of Ostia) has made the things mentioned at its own expense

The end of the text was probably identical to that on his statue base on the Forum (see no 16). Vincentius reused a statue base from the Square of the Guilds, now in front of the Theatre (see no 7). He was active between AD 385 and 389.

Around 127 inscribed objects were reused in the floors of the baths in the late 4th century. They came from the Forum, guild buildings and cemeteries among other places. One of the most interesting inscriptions, on a plaster cast of a marble tablet now exhibited on the north wall of the second tepidarium, may refer to the placing of an altar for wedding rites. It is dated after 140 or 141 when Faustina was deified. The text reads (*CIL* XIV S 5326):

DECURIONUM DECRETO
IMP(eratori) CAESARI T(ito) AELIO HADRIANO ANTONINO AUG(usto) PIO P(atri) P(atriae)
ET DIVAE FAUSTINAE OB INSIGNEM EORUM CONCORDIAM UTIQUE IN ARA VIRGINES QUAE IN COLONIA OSTIENS(i) NUBENT
ITEM MARITI EARUM SUPPLICENT

By decree of the town councillors. For Imperator Titus Aelius Hadrianus Antoninus Augustus Pius, father of the fatherland, and for (his wife) the divine Faustina, because of their harmony and in order that virgins who marry in the Colonia Ostiensis *at the altar, (and) in the same way their husbands, would utter their supplications*

The text suggests that couples should behave just as harmoniously as the emperor Antoninus Pius and his wife did. Those who married did not say yes to each other; usually the bride asked the bridegroom to accept her as his wife. Women could marry around 14 years of age. Funerary inscriptions show that preserving one's virginity until the wedding was appreciated.

19. THE STOREHOUSE OF EPAGATHUS AND EPAPHRODITUS
(HORREA EPAGATHIANA; I, viii, 3)

Above the monumental entrance to this large storehouse with a central, open court, along the Via Epigathiana, is a marble *tabula ansata* (tablet with handles) with the following inscription (*CIL* XIV S 4709):

| HORREA EPAGATHIANA ET EPAPHRODITIANA | *Storehouse of Epagathus and Epaphroditus* |

The storehouse is dated to ca AD 137-138. The two owners were freedmen as their surnames are of Greek origin. The Greek adjectives *ep-agathos* and *ep-aphroditos* mean belonging to Good (Fortune; compare Greek *Agathē Tychē*: Good Luck) and belonging to Aphrodite respectively. Unfortunately their family names are unknown. The building was constructed in the 130s. The monumental double entrance, the second featuring large travertine doorposts, indicates that expensive goods, possibly spices, were stored here. Also, the staircase in the vestibule could be closed. The goods may have been distributed to retail traders. At the other side of the court are two niches. They may have held statuettes of *Agathē Tychē* (Fortuna) and *Aphrodite* (Venus) if these deities were indeed the protectors of the owners or the stored goods. Niches of this type and small cult rooms are often present in deposits, workshops and houses.

20. THE BATHS OF BUTICOSUS (TERME DI BUTICOSO; I, xiv, 8)

These private baths (*balnea*), possibly the property of a guild, opposite the Horrea Epigathiana, are small and inserted between shops. On the evidence of brick stamps they can be dated between AD 112 and 115, in the period of Trajan. The black-and-white mosaic in the vestibule depicts fancy sea monsters and a nude bath master or superintendent holding a bucket and perhaps a *strigilis*. A strigil is an instrument to cleanse the body of oil and dirt after boxing or wrestling (see no 3). The inscription reads (*AE* 1940, 42; *fig. 24*):

| EPICTETUS BVTICOSUS | *Epictetus Buticosus* |

The (removed) wall-paintings show gardens, a common theme in bath buildings of the 2nd and 3rd centuries AD.

Fig. 24. Mosaic in the Baths of Buticosus (photo author).

21. THE SACRED AREA OF THE HERCULES TEMPLE
(AREA SACRA REPUBBLICANA; I, xv, 1-6)

The sanctuary, along the Via della Foce, has one large, almost east-oriented temple, dedicated to Hercules, dated to ca 90 BC, and small temples on the left and right, one of which may have been dedicated to Liber Pater (Dionysus), god of the wine and one which was almost certainly dedicated to Asclepius, the god of healing. It lies circa one metre below street level which indicates that the city wanted to preserve a place of old traditions and memories in its ancient form.

In the *cella* of the Hercules temple (near the rear wall) is an almost square base of white Greek marble with an inscription that reads (*AE* 1971, 71):

P(ublius) . LIVIUS . P(ublii) L(ibertus) . HER(culi) . DA(t)

Publius Livius, freedman of Publius, gives (this) to Hercules

The block is one of the oldest pieces of imported Greek marble in Ostia, and dates between ca 150 and 80 BC.

A copy of the famous *haruspex* relief is attached to a wall on the left. The original of Penthelic marble is in the local museum. The left part is missing. The relief is dated to ca 90-65 BC based on the length of the togas and the Republican spelling of the word *haruspexs*. The three scenes should be 'read' from right to left:

1. Fishermen draw a net ashore that holds not only fish but also an archaic, armoured statue of the Greek demi-god Hercules and a little chest. In Hercules' right hand the handle of a club is visible.
2. A large, bearded, identically armoured man holding a club in his left hand, has taken an inscribed oracle lot (sors) from the chest, which stands on a base and is handing it over to a boy in toga. In view of the attribute that man is Hercules once more, but now in action. The large diptych above may be an opened lot, rendered at an enlarged scale.
3. An adult man in toga, probably the haruspex C. Fulvius Salvis himself, a seer, gives the lot to what might be a military commander, possibly of a fleet (not visible). Victoria, personification of the victory, hovers over the scene. So the consultation predicted success.

The centralized inscription reads (*AE* 1971, 72; *fig. 25* (from G. Becatti, *BollCom* 67, 1939)):

C(aius) FULVIUS SALVIS HARUSPEXS D(onum) D(edit)

Gaius Fulvius Salvis, haruspex, *has given (this relief) as gift*

On the lot in Hercules' hand is written:

[S]ORT(es) H(erculis)　　　　　　　　　　　　　　*Oracle lots of Hercules*

The statue of Hercules was fished up from the sea near or at the Tiber mouth. This miraculous catch must have been a lucky omen. It may have been the reason why a temple was dedicated to him. A *haruspex* is an Etruscan seer who interpreted the livers of sacrificial animals (usually sheep), lightning and omens. Occasionally he could also divine by using lots. In

Fig. 25. Relief found near the Hercules temple (Becatti 1939).

Tibur (modern Tivoli) Hercules was associated with oracles too. In the sanctuary of Fortuna Primigenia in Praeneste (modern Palestrina) to the southeast of Rome, a *puer* (boy) descended into a pit in order to take a lot from it. It is not impossible that Etruscan seers adopted Italic and Roman oracle practices. Fulvius' surname Salvis is attested as a family name in Etruscan inscriptions from Perugia.

Interestingly, a small marble altar dedicated to Hercules, dating to the reign of Augustus, was placed upside down and reused in the small *Mithraeum* in the rear of the House of Diana (I, iii, 4; closed for the public) around AD 250. It was perforated horizontally so that it could contain an oil lamp. The original lies in the *cella* of the Hercules temple. The inscription on its front reads (*CIL* XIV S 4280):

AQUAE SALVIAE	*To the Salvian Water (and)*
HERCLI SAC(rum)	*to Herc(u)les sacred*

The inscription on the left side is almost similar: AQVA SALVIA / HERCLI SAC. The first words are now written in the nominative.

The female adjective Salvia may be akin to the *cognomen* of the *haruspex*, Salvis. He may, as water diviner (*aquilex*), have detected sweet underground water. The Italic Hercules is known as protector of water. So the altar may originate from the Hercules sanctuary, representing a fragment of the altar that was found near the Forum. The secondary inscription on the back of the altar mentions a Marcus Lollianus Callinicus, a *pater* (main priest) who gave the altar to the god (Mithras) (*CIL* XIV S 4310; ca AD 250). Callinicus (Gr. *kallinikos*: 'beautiful winner') is a well known epithet of Heracles, possibly a coincidence.

In the forepart (*pars antica*) of the large temple stands an altar or base with the following inscription on its front (*AE* 1948, 126; *fig. 26*):

DEO
INVICTO HERCULI
HOSTILIUS ANTIPATER
 V(ir) P(erfectissimus) PRAEF(ectus) ANN(onae)
 CURAT(or) REI PUBLIC(ae) OST(iensis)

For the invincible god Hercules. Hostilius Antipater, a very perfect man, chief of the grain supply, curator of the city of Ostia

Hostilius Antipater was active during the reign of Diocletian, at the end of the third century AD. In the first decennia of the fourth century the title VP went out of use. The altar was a reused statue base, placed upside down as is shown by the older, partly erased inscription on the back (*AE* 1955, 175; *fig. 27*). It mentions Publius Flavius Priscus who lived around 249 (see also no 7, base no 6). The reversed base has a deep, cylindrical hole, which may have held sacred water.

Fig. 26. Altar (reused base) in the Hercules temple (photo author).

Fig. 27. Altar (reused base) in the Hercules temple. Back (photo author).

On the travertine stairs of the temple stands a plaster copy of the marble statue (original now in the local museum), which was erected for Gaius Cartilius Poplicola, one of the most important and popular men of Ostia. He was active in the late Republican period and during the early reign of the emperor Augustus. His mausoleum, next to the ancient seashore, is dealt with under no 28. The statue was sculpted between ca 40 and 30 BC. It bears the following inscription (*AE* 1971, 74):

C(aius) CARTILIUS C(ai) F(ilius)	*Gaius Cartilius, son of Gaius,*
DUOVIRU TERTIO	*duovir for the third time*
POPLICOLAE	*for Poplicola*

The original text was:

C(aius) CARTILIUS C(aii) F(ilius)	*Gaius Cartilius, son of Gaius,*
DUOVIR ITERUM	*mayor for the second time*

When Cartilius became mayor for the third time, the word ITERUM was overwritten by TERTIO and the surname POPLICOLA, friend of the people, was added, incorrectly in the dative case.

The honorary statue was an adapted copy of a Greek statue from the 4th century BC, which probably represented Neptune with a trident. Only the head, now lost, was Roman. This type of hybrid, composite statues, demonstrating the combination of classicism and realism, was made by Neo-Attic sculptors (originally from Athens) for Roman patrons, not only on Delos but also in Italy (see also no 22).

22. THE MITHRAEUM UNDER THE BATHS OF MITHRAS
(TERME DEL MITRA; I, xvii, 2)

The monumental Baths of Mithras along the Via della Foce, built around AD 125 with several later facelifts, have enormous subterranean spaces. The underground *Mithraeum* can be entered from the northeast side (*fig. 28*). It is a sacred space dedicated to Mithras, a deity of Persian origin. This rectangular, vaulted space (*spelaeum* (cave); *templum*), dated to ca AD 200, harbours two series of long stone benches on both sides (*praesepia*) of the corridor. Originally the vaults imitated the heaven, depicting painted stars. The initiated men belonged to seven grades (see no 40), who reclined in a hierarchical order. The lowest initiates reclined near the entrance, the highest at the far end of the corridor. Some initiates may have worn animal masks (raven, lion) during their mysterious meetings. At the far end of the sacred space, behind a triangular altar and a square base, stands a diagonally placed plaster copy of a marble statue group representing Mithras about to kill a bull (the original is in the local museum). The mythical killing (*taurobolium*) generated new life, as can often be seen in Mithraic reliefs and paintings: among others a wheat ear arises from the bull's tail (see no 40). For practical reasons, the initiates did not consume a bull but ate small animals, chickens and other birds, and drank wine.

Fourteen *Mithraea* have been discovered in Ostia so far. They were built between ca 160 and 250. In the final phase they are spread all over the city. Most of them are rather hidden in the rear of buildings or open courts, as the cult had an exclusive, male-focused, mysterious character.

The Greek inscription on the neck of the bull reads (*SEG* 13, 476):

ΚΡΙΤΩΝ	*Kriton*
ΑΘΗΝΑΙΟΣ	*the Athenian*
ΕΠΟΙΕΙ	*made (me)*
(transcription: Kritōn Athēnaios epoiei)	

The group was made by a sculptor of the Neo-Attic school, not without

*Fig. 28. Mithraeum under the Baths of Mithras
(photo Maarten van Deventer).*

the typical Hellenistic pathos. It is usually dated to the 2nd century AD. Kriton may be identical to the Marcus Umbilius Criton known from a votive marble basin (*labrum*) found in the Mithraeum of Planta Pedis, to the west of the Serapeum (see no 26). He became a freedman thanks to a senator, Marcus Umbilius Maximus, who was probably *patronus* of an Ostian guild in AD 192. A son of the latter was honoured with a statue in the Serapeum (see no 26).

The statue group was probably heavily damaged by Christians, because above, inside the Baths, a room with an apse was built to serve as a Christian chapel or oratory around 400. Obviously, it was meant to be an act of victory over and damnation of memory of the pagan religion. Part of the Baths may have been used for baptizing. Two small plaster pillars, copies of the marble originals (height 132 cm), in front of the chapel, bear the following characters:

XP (the *chrismon*, Chi - Rho, intertwined, in Greek characters: Christus) between A and Ω (Alpha and Omega, the first and last character of the Greek alphabet)

The message is clear: Christ is the beginning and the end as stated in the

New Testament (*Revelation* 1, 8). Lateral grooves in the pillars show that a fence once stood between the pillars. It may have been a choir-screen.

23. THE HALL OF THE GRAIN MEASURERS
(AULA DEI MENSORES; I, xix, 3)

The square hall is ca 50 cm above street level, to the left of the Temple of the Guild of the Grain Measurers (*corpus mensorum frumentariorum*), along the Via della Foce. Behind these buildings are *horrea* ('storehouses'), probably for storing grain (I, xiv, 4).

The black-and-white mosaic in the hall, dated to ca AD 235, shows six men in a rectangular frame, from left to right: a frontal man and a porter carrying a sack of grain (*saccarius*), a boy raising the index finger of his right hand, holding a lead staff with ten branches (*coduli*) for strips (*tesserae*) indicating the number of 9 filled *modii*, and three men standing around a large *modius* (tapering, cylindrical vessel). One holds a *rutellum*, a rod to level off the grain at the top of the *modius*, one man has an emptied sack and another man makes a demonstrative gesture, suggesting that 'the job is finished'. A *modius* had a capacity of ca 9 litres (6.503 kg). The fragmentary inscription reads (Becatti 1961, p. 35; *fig. 29*):

V[….]SEXHAGIHI
Reconstructed by G. Becatti as:
V[ILICI] SEX H(orreorum) AGI(lianorum) HI(c)

Six superintendents of the granary of the Agilii (are) here.

Vilici horreorum are known from Rome. The reconstruction is, however, not convincing as not all six persons are overseers. After the letter V there is space for four letters. Another possible reconstruction is VIRI (men). In other inscriptions the word *horrea* is abbreviated as H (e.g.: *AE* 1924, 36). *Horrea* often have the name of proprietors. The suggestion that the initial words were numerals indicating the amount of grain (*AE* 2004, 364) is incorrect as the Latin word *frumentum* (grain) is absent.

The mosaic shows shadows under some feet, which is characteristic of third century mosaics.

The inscription on a fragmentary marble statue base in the same hall reads (Becatti 1961, p. 35):

Fig. 29. Mosaic in the Hall of the Grain Measurers (photo author).

        [---]IMO
        [---]STATUAM
   [---]LAURENTIO V(iro) P(erfectissimo)
[--- PATRO]NO CORPOR(is) MENSOR(u)M
[--- [O]B CONTEMPLATIONEM EMERITOR(um)
[--- [UNIV]ERSUM CORPUS ANIMIS EXULTANTIBUS
[--- [DIGN]ITISSIMO COLLOCAVIT

... *statue (obj.) for the patron of the Guild of the Measurers, Laurentius, a very perfect man, the whole guild (subj.) in view of his merits with excitement for a dignified man has placed*

The abbreviated honorary title VP (*vir perfectissimus*) predominated around 300 AD (see no 21). The words *animis exultantibus* occur in ancient Christian literature but they do not prove that this guild was Christian around that date.

The Temple of the Guild was probably dedicated to Ceres Augusta, the imperial Ceres, tutelary deity of agriculture and grain (see *CIL* XIV 409).

24. THE BATHS OF THE SEVEN WISE MEN
(TERME DEI SETTE SAPIENTI; III, x, 2)

This impressive bath complex is Hadrianic in date. It has a large circular room, originally the cold water bath (*frigidarium*) with a splendid, black-and-white mosaic depicting hunting scenes and vegetal motifs. The restoration is ancient. A second *frigidarium* at a lower level harbours a painting of Venus rising from the sea. Little Amores around her hold toilet articles. Just to the left of the monumental entrance with stucco reliefs of bull-heads (*bucrania*) there is a dressing room, which previously, in the time of Trajan, was a room for the consumption of wine as may be deduced from three painted *amphorae* (one labeled: FALERNVM) and a hovering man holding a *cantharus*, clear references to Bacchus. Falernum was a famous Campanian wine. Another Ostian funerary inscription (*CIL* XIV 914) lists it together with the other joys of life: *balnea*, *vina*, *Venus* ('baths, wines, and love'; also mentioned in *CIL* VI 15258). The wall paintings, dated between AD 126 and 160, show two rows of men. The upper row shows four of the Seven Sages, sitting on chairs. To the left and right of each Sage, we see a fragmentary painted inscription in Latin (…ENIS BIAS), and four Greek names:

[…]ENIS BIAS
COΛΩN AΘHNAIOC ΘAΛHC MEIΛHCIOC XEIΛΩN ΛAKEΔAIMONIOC [....] ΠPIHNEUC

Transcription: Solōn Athēnaios   Thalēs Meilēsios   Cheilōn Lakedaimonios   [....] Priēneus

Solon of Athens   Thales of Miletus   Cheilon of Sparta   (Bias) of Priene

Above their heads are the following texts in metric verses, iambic *senarii* (*AE* 1941, 4):

UT BENE CACARET VENTREM PALPAVIT SOLON

In order to ease nature Solon rubbed his belly

DURUM CACANTES MONUIT UT NITANT THALES

Those who had problems with easing nature Thales advised to take a firm stand

VISSIRE TACITE CHILON DOCUIT SUBDOLUS

Cheilon taught, smart as he was, to fart softly

Under the Sages was another row of men. Only their heads and the following texts are visible (*AE* 1941, 8):

PROPERA *Make haste!*

AGITA TE CELERIUS   *Move faster and you will be ready quicker!*
PERVENIES

AMICE FUGIT TE PROVERBIUM
BENE CACA ET IRRIMA MEDICOS

Friend: does the proverb escape you: ease nature and fuck your physicians?

The Seven Wise Men who lived around 600 BC did not pay attention to problems of (in)digestion. They were famous for one-liners, e.g. Solon's 'nothing too much (keep measure)', Cheilon's 'know yourself' and Bias' 'most people are bad'. The paintings of the other Sages, probably Kleoboulos of Lindos, Periandros of Corinth, and Pittakos of Lesbos, have not been preserved.

In the 1st century AD Plutarch, in his book *The Dinner of the Seven Wise Men*, did associate the Seven Sages with eating and drinking. The Sages were obviously reinterpreted in a Roman way. According to S. Mols the metric Latin texts above the Wise Men may originate from burlesque theatre plays. If true, they ridicule members of the Roman elite who associated themselves, be it in a rather realistic way, with the Seven Sages.

A black-and-white mosaic in the room between the *frigidarium* and *caldarium*, dated to ca AD 205, shows a tall nude man in frontal position probably holding a staff in his left hand. The inscription above him reads (*fig. 30*):

IULI (ivy leaf) CARDI H(ic) C(onspicitur) E(ffigies)

Of Julius Cardus here is watched (his) image (Here Julius Cardus' image can be seen)

Julius Cardus may have been the bath-master (*balneator*).

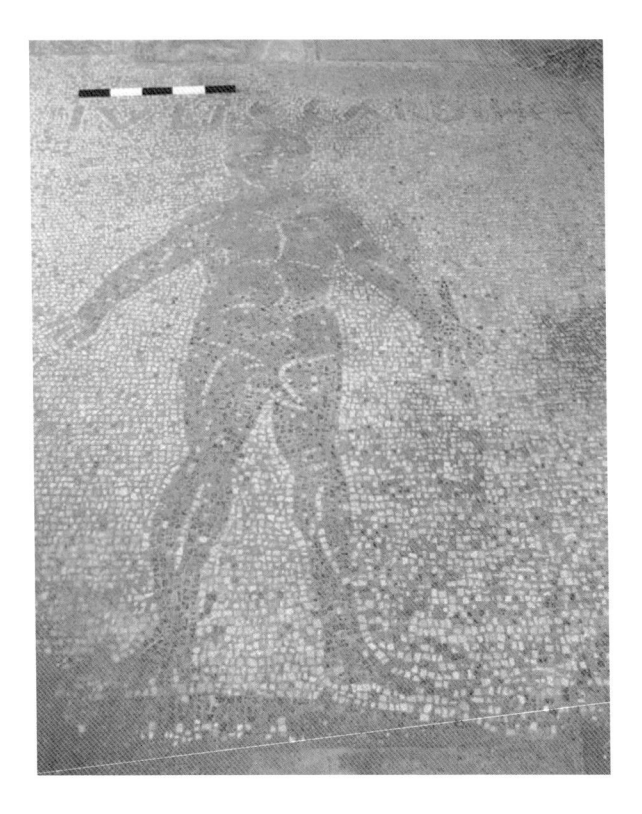

Fig. 30. Mosaic in the Baths of the Seven Wise Men (photo author).

25. THE BATHS OF TRINACRIA (TERME DI TRINACRIA; III, xvi, 7)

These private baths date to the time of Hadrian (AD 117-138). A mosaic near the entrance (to the right) shows a female bust with three human legs on its head. It symbolizes Sicily. This island has a triangular form. In Greek it is called *Triskeles* ('three legs') and in Latin *Trinacria* ('three corners').

The next L-shaped room, a *tepidarium* or *caldarium*, has black-and-white mosaics featuring sea animals and an inscription that reads (Becatti 1961, p. 141; *fig. 31*):

STATIO CUNNULINGIORUN   *Office of the cunt lickers*
(that is: *statio cunnulingiorun > cunnilingiorum*)

It is dated to the second half of the 2nd century AD. It could only be read by those sitting on a bench along the wall. Possibly the side-room served

Fig. 31. Mosaic in the Baths of Trinacria (photo author).

as a brothel. A brothel in the form of an independent building has been found in Pompeii but not in Ostia so far. Prostitution probably took place in hotels, bars and baths. In this case male prostitutes may have offered their services to female visitors. The practice, which commanded a very low price, shows up in Pompeian graffiti and is illustrated in a painting in the *apodyterium* (undressing room) of the Suburban Baths at Pompeii. On the other hand *cunnilingus* had a bad reputation in the Roman world (see also no 15). The position and reading direction of the inscription make the possibility that this was a joke, a paraphrase of the *statio* inscriptions in the Square of the Guilds (see no 7) and elsewhere in Ostia, less likely.

Another room has a splendid mosaic showing dolphins and a Nereid riding on a bull with a fishtail.

M(arco) UMBILIO M(arci) F(ilio) ARN(ensi)
        MAXIMINO
PRAETEXTATO C(larissimo) P(uero) P(atrono) C(oloniae)
        SACERDOTI GENI COL(oniae)
        P(ublius) CALPURNIUS
        PRINCEPS EQUO PUBL(ico)
OMNIBUS HONORIBUS FUNCTUS
        EDUCATOR

For Marcus Umbilius Maximinus, son of Marcus, from (the tribus*) Arnensis, a very renowned boy, wearing a toga with a purple hem, patron of the* colonia*, priest of the Genius of the* colonia*, Publius Calpurnius Princeps, honoured with the public horse, having fulfilled all magistracies, educator (erected this statue)*

On the right side:

DEDICATA K(alendis) MARTI(i)S
SEVERO ET VICTORINO CO(n)S(ulibus)

(Base/statue) dedicated on 1 March, when Severus and Victorinus were consuls

Severus and Victorinus were consuls in AD 200. Marcus Umbilius was not of Ostian origin. Publius Calpurnius was a teacher. Judging by the context he may have been a priest who taught and initiated people into the secrets of the Serapis cult. The left side of the base features a pitcher, the right side a *patera umbilicata* (dish with navel). Opposite the base is another, similar one, without inscription. It shows again that inscriptions could be made on the spot.

Statues of Serapis also stood elsewhere in the city. Marcus Minucius Felix, a Christian author who lived between ca AD 150 and 222, describes how his and Octavius' pagan friend Quintus Caecilius made a gesture of adoration in front of a Serapis statue (*Octavius* 2.3):

>…*placuit Ostiam petere, amoenissimam civitatem, quod esset corpori meo siccandis umoribus de marinis lavacris blanda et adposita curatio: sane et ad vindemiam feriae iudiciariam curam relaxaverant. Nam id temporis post aestivam diem in temperiem semet autumnitas dirigebat. (4) Itaque cum diluculo ad mare inambulando litori (litore) pergeremus, ut et aura adspirans leniter membra vegetaret et cum eximia voluptate molli vestigio cedens*

harena subsideret, Caecilius simulacro Serapidis denotato, ut vulgus superstitiosus solet, manum ori admovens osculum labiis pressit…

…we decided to visit Ostia, a very lovely city, because it would be an agreeable and fitting treatment for my body by drying the humours from the sea baths. The feast days of the wine harvest had ended the judicial duties. For the autumn brought, after the summer heat, a cooler temperature. So when we were going to the seashore by walking up and down so that the breeze refreshed our limbs and the sand gave way to our feet causing great pleasure, Caecilius noticed a statue of Serapis, moved his hand to his lips with a kiss and pressed a kiss onto it like the superstitious mob uses to do…

Other ancient texts show that an adorant raised his right hand to his lips. In fact it was intended as a blown kiss in the direction of an inaccessible statue rather than kissing the statue itself. Serapis statues were very popular in the Roman world. The Christian author Tertullian (*Ad nationes* 2.8) who lived in the second century, writes: 'the whole earth swears to Serapis.'

The environment of the Serapeum also exhibits Egyptian elements. Several Serapis inscriptions, some of which are written in Greek, have been found in the neighbourhood. In the courtyard of the monumental flat building now called Caseggiato del Serapide (III, x, 3), dated to AD 126-127, is a shrine (*aedicula*) featuring a statue of Serapis sitting on a throne, dating to the Severan period. The Mithraeum of Planta Pedis (III, xvii, 2; ca AD 200) harbours a footprint in terracotta, which is an uncommon votive gift in *Mithraea* but common in Egyptian sanctuaries. The complex of the Garden Houses (III, ix; c. AD 128), a kind of gated community, has six *nymphaea* (fountains) in its surrounding garden, one of which featured a mosaic showing a Nilotic scene. These data suggest that grain merchants from Egypt may have lived in *Regio* III in the second century. To the north of the Sanctuary were *horrea*, probably grainstores, which have not yet been excavated.

27. The House of Annius (Casa di Annio; III, xiv, 4)

Thanks to brick stamps the building can be dated to AD 128-129, the time of Hadrian. It has shops along the street. The house belonged to a certain Annius. Only his family name is known. Three terracotta slabs on the curved part of a pseudo-balcony are inscribed (*fig. 32*):

OMNIA   FELICI[A]   ANNI

(May) all business of Annius (be) lucky (or: All business (are going) well)

Fig. 32. The House of Annius (photo author).

The text probably represents a wish rather than a statement. Similar texts occur in house mosaics elsewhere in the Roman world: *omnia tibi felicia* ('may all go well with you!').

Below the inscriptions to the left and to the right are two terracotta slabs with reliefs. One depicts a merchant behind a wooden table on two trestles and one large vessel (*dolium*) in the foreground, the other a sailboat with a helmsman. Annius may, therefore, have fulfilled two functions. Similar terracotta slabs are in or have been found on the facades of tombs at Isola Sacra, the cemetery of Portus. Some tombs also provide evidence of two jobs.

The adjacent House of the Dolia (Caseggiato dei Dolii; III, xiv, 3) may have belonged to Annius.

28. THE HOUSE OF THE THUNDERBOLT (*DOMUS FULMINATA*; III, VII, 3)

This building, outside the Porta Marina, dated between AD 65 and 75, has shops and bars along the street. Passing through a central corridor, next to a travertine staircase, one enters a peristyle which has two cisterns and a *biclinium*, two parallel stone couches. A base which once supported a marble altar from the time of Augustus (now lost) stands between them. Behind the couches is an *aedicula*, a small chapel with an opening at ground level, perhaps imitating a tomb. The building is connected with the contemporaneous enclosing wall of the space around the adjacent mausoleum, built ca 35-30 BC, possibly for Publius Lucilius Gamala ('senior'; see no 9 and Appendix 3) who, just like Gaius Cartilius Poplicola (see no 29), was one the most famous of Ostia's inhabitants. The mausoleum is at a far lower level than the House of the Thunderbolt. The latter may have been built by P. Lucilius Gamala, a descendent of Gamala 'senior', who was *duovir* (mayor) in AD 71. The two stone couches may have been used to commemorate Gamala 'senior' with funerary meals. To the left of the peristyle is the residential area with a toilet with three seats and an internal staircase leading to the upper floor. The doors between residence and peristyle could only be opened from the residential area. To the right of the peristyle are rooms with originally high ceilings and a corner room probably used as a winter dining room.

In the left rear corner of the peristyle is a small rectangular burial mound, a modern reconstruction of a *tumulus* (mound) with a very small marble tablet bearing the inscription FDC (*AE* 1946, 188; 1947, 13):

F(ulgur) D(ium) C(onditum)   *A divine thunderbolt (has been) buried*

A location that was struck by a thunderbolt was provided with a ritual tomb containing all the objects which had been damaged and turned into a mound. It was consecrated by a *haruspex* (Etruscan seer interpreting lightning, entrails (livers) and omens), or a *sacerdos bidentalis* (see *CIL* XIV 188; S 5340) or by assistants (*aedilicii*) of Ostia's most important priest, the *pontifex Volkani*, high priest of Vulcanus (see *CIL* XIV 245). Another unabbreviated Ostian inscription mentions: FVLGUR DIUM (*AE* 1913, 218).

29. The Tomb of C. Cartilius Poplicola (IV, ix, 2)

The second mausoleum outside Porta Marina, near the former, ancient shoreline, has a marble front, travertine sides and a tuff rear wall. It bears a monumental inscription (*AE* 1968, 82; *fig. 33*):

PUBLICE

C(aio) CARTILIO C(ai) F(ilio) POPLICOLAE [DUOVIRO VIII…] ......
             LIBEREIS POS[TERISQUE EIUS]
[DECURIONUM DECRETO CO]LONORUMQUE CON[SENSU]

Fig. 33. The Tomb of C. Publicius Poplicola (photo author).

PREIMARIO VIRO PRO EIUS MERITEIS
HOC MONUMENTUM CONSTITUTUM EST
 EIQUE MERENTI GRATIA RELLATA EST
ISQUE OCTIENS DUOMVIR TER CENS(or) COLONORUM IUDICIO
 APSENS PRAESENSQUE FACTUS EST
OB EIUS AMOREM IN UNIVERSOS AB
 UNIVERSIEIS [---]

                HUMANIAE M(arci) F(iliae)

At public expense

For Gaius Cartilius Poplicola, son of Gaius, eight times duovir *('mayor'), and for his children and offspring this monument is founded by decree of the town councillors and with the approval of the citizens for an excellent man because of his merits and because he deserves it, thanks are given to him. And he was made duomvir eight times in presence and absence, and three times censor by the judgement of the citizens. Because of his love for everybody, by everybody ....[he was honoured?]*

For Humania, daughter of Marcus

The monument for the popular Ostian mayor was built around 20-15 BC, during the early part of Augustus' reign (see no 21). Sixteen *fasces* (iron rods) are visible above the inscription. They were carried by *lictores* who had to protect the *duovir*. Two rods symbolize one administrative year. The adverb *publice* can also mean: in name of the city.

The marble frieze crowning the monument at the front shows the imminent attack by sea pirates. To the left infantrymen are led by a person who is larger than them, probably Cartilius himself, and to the right is a war ship with a prow in the form of the head of Minerva. A warrior standing on the ship is about to throw a spear. Evidently Cartilius is leading his men to ward off the enemy fleet. By his diplomacy the conflict is resolved. He forbids the soldiers to attack the ship. Probably the scene illustrates a raid on Ostia by Sextus Pompeius in 40 or 39 BC. Cartilius may have earned his surname Poplicola ('Friend of the People'), because he saved Ostia.

The Humania mentioned in the last line was probably his wife. The Cartilius family may have originated from Chiusi in North Etruria.

30. THE SANCTUARY OF BONA DEA (SANTUARIO DI BONA DEA; IV, viii, 3)

This curious suburban sanctuary, outside the Ciceronian city wall, near Porta Marina, dates to ca AD 40. It retained its function until the 3rd or 4th century AD, albeit eventually in a reduced form because a water basin was constructed on the street side. It is one of the two sanctuaries dedicated to the fertility goddess Bona Dea (Good Goddess). The modern plaster copy of one of the three, but possibly six, identical marble building inscriptions reads (*AE* 1946, 221; *fig. 34*):

M(arcus) MAECIL[I]US M(arci) F(ilius) [F]URR[(ianus)] DUOVIR AEDEM BONAE DEA[E] EX SU[A PECUNIA FAC(iendam) CUR(avit)] IDEMQ(ue) PRO[BAVIT]

Marcus Maecilius Furrianus, son of Marcus, mayor, had the Temple of Bona

Fig. 34. Inscription in the Sanctuary of Bona Dea, copy (photo author).

Dea built at his own expense and the same man has approved (it)

The family name Maecilius and surname Furrianus (formerly incorrectly restored as [T]urranius) are known from Rome but not from other Ostian inscriptions. So probably the cult was introduced from Rome. Marcus' inscriptions are a clear example of self-representation.

There is uncertainty about the identity of the goddess. Some ancient authors call her daughter of Faunus. One version of the myth records that he fell in love with her. She refused his advances, after which he tried to get her drunk. When she still resisted, Faunus changed himself into a snake and had intercourse with her. She remained chaste, however. She never left the women's room of her house. So she was never seen by another man. Probably as a consequence men did not have access to her sanctuary (for the story of an intrusive man, see no 2). The walls of her sanctuary were so high that nobody could see what was happening inside. For the same reason the temple did not have a podium. But as the inscriptions show, a man could act as benefactor, in this case by financing the temple (*aedes*).

In the neighbourhood a statue of snake curling around a phallus was found. This may point to fertility although snakes can also be associated with healing as is the case with the snake of Asclepius. The presence of a counter may indicate the distribution of drugs by priestesses; we know that this happened in the temple of Bona Dea on the Aventine in Rome.

The goddess was multifunctional. She was probably an old Italic fertility goddess. She protected land, cattle and owners. Fertility and healing are closely related. In later periods she became, possibly under oriental influences, a kind of 'all'-goddess.

The other, late-Republican Bona Dea sanctuary is inside the city walls, in *Regio* V, x, 2, far below street level. An inscription on a travertine slab (not in situ) reads (*AE* 2004, 361):

OCTAVIA M F GAMALAE
  PORTIC(um) POLIEND(am)
  ET SEDEILIA FACIUN(da)
  ET CULINA(m) TEGEND(am)
  D(eae) B(onae) CURAVIT

Octavia, daughter of Marcus, wife of Gamala,
had the portico plastered, and the seats made, and the kitchen covered for the Good Goddess

This Octavia was probably the wife of the famous Publius Lucilius Gamala (see nos 21 and 29). Her benefaction may have taken place between ca 70 and 60 BC.

31. THE BAR OF ALEXANDER AND HELIX
(CAUPONA DI ALEXANDER; IV, vii, 4)

The corner building, on the site of Porta Marina, dates to the Antonine period (after AD 138). It was built along the *decumanus*, against the Ciceronian city wall and gate. First it was a shop (*taberna*), then, in the late Severan period (ca 210-235), it became a bar. The black-and-white mosaic shows among others two pancratiasts with their names (Becatti 1961, p. 206; *fig. 35*):

ALEXANDER   HELIX

The athletes have been identified by C.P. Jones as Gaius Perelius Aurelius Alexander and Aurelius Helix, both famous pancratiasts during the reign

26. The Serapeum (Serapeo; III, xvii, 4)

Whoever enters the Sanctuary of the Egyptian god Serapis sees on the right marble slabs with the inscription (*AE* 1956, 76):

IOVI SERAPI   *To Jupiter Serapis*

The slabs belonged to the pediment of the vestibule, which covered part of the pavement. They date to the 2nd century AD. They were reused in late antiquity in the pavement of the courtyard in front of the temple.

Serapis is an Egyptian god, a mix of Osiris and Apis, probably created on the initiative of Ptolemaeus II in Alexandria around 300 BC. Statues of this deity betray Greek elements, among others the addition of Cerberus, the dog of the underworld. Evidently in Ostia, the upper god Jupiter among others was assimilated with Serapis. A fragment of the *Fasti Ostienses*, the local year calendar, listing the names of the most important magistrates and events at Rome and at Ostia, mentions that the temple was dedicated in AD 127:

…VIIII K(alendas) FEBR(uarias) TEMPLUM SARAPI QUOD [.] CALTILIUS P[---] SUA PECUNIA EXSTRUXIT DEDICATUM [ES]T…

…on the ninth day before the first day of February the temple for Sarapis that [.] Caltilius P[---] has (had) built at his own expense, has been dedicated…

This date, 24 January, was the birthday (*dies natalis*) of Hadrian who was emperor in 127. The word *Kalendae* indicates the first day of a month. Brick stamps date the building of the temple to between 123 and 126. Owner of the brick work (*dominus figlinae*) was Annius Verus, who was prefect of Rome in 120 and consul for the third time in 126. Responsible for the building of the temple was an otherwise unknown member of the family of the Caltilii. Votive objects were given by members of the Statilii (freedmen), with inscriptions in Latin and Greek (Stateilios).

The floor of the entrance is paved with a black-and-white mosaic depicting the Apis bull. The floor of the courtyard in front of the temple harbours a Nile mosaic. On the right is a statue base. The inscription on the front reads (*AE* 1988, 214):

Fig. 35. Mosaic in the Bar of Alexander and Helix (photo author).

of the emperor Heliogabalus (218-222). The *pancration* was a combination of boxing and wrestling. Neither man is shown as boxing as they do not wear leather thongs (*caestus*). Between them is a palm leaf, sign of victory, and to the right a metal footed bowl, the prize for the winner. A contemporary mosaic in the *apodyterium* (undressing room) of the *palaestra* (wrestling court) of the baths belonging to a suburban villa near Puteoli (Pozzuoli) depicts four pugilists (now in Museo archeologico dei Campi Flegrei, Baia; *fig. 36*). The preserved inscriptions mention: Elix, Magira, and Alexander. In the *tabulata ansata* we read ISEO / EUSEBEIA. The second word refers to posthumous games in honour of Hadrian.

Helix was victor in the Greek-style Capitolian games (*Capitolia*) in Rome in AD 218. These games, which were instituted by Domitian in 86 and organised until the 4th century, combined musical, equestrian and gymnastic competitions. His opponent Alexander, originating from Asia Minor, was so famous that he became an ambassador of Heliogabalus; a nice parallel for the Dutch judo practicioner Anton Geesink who acted as a cultural ambassador of the Netherlands. Magira has been identified by J.-Y. Strasser as the famous pancratiast Aurelios Zotikos Mageiros from Smyrna. His surname means 'cook' or 'butcher' (the latter possibly in light of his sexual activities). His Latin surname, Magira, is female which may be attributable to his homoerotic relations, especially with Heliogabalus.

Fig. 36. Mosaic from the baths of a villa near Pozzuoli (photo Patrick Gouw).

Of course Alexander and Helix were not the proprietors of the Ostian pub. The owner and his clients must have been fascinated by the universal fame of or by a performance of the two.

Other Ostian mosaics showing athletes are located in the Baths of Neptune, the Baths of Trinacria, the Baths of the Sea (Terme maritime), in the House of Apuleius showing MUSCLOSUS, a famous charioteer in Rome, the Caseggiato dei Lottatori showing ARTEMI(dorus) as victor and SACAL[---] as defeated, the Baths of Trinacria (see no 25), the Terme of the so-called Palazzo Imperiale (lost mosaic), the Terme Marittime, the Baths of Porta Marina, and the Baths on the Via Severiana (lost mosaic). The latter depicts busts of athletes labelled with nicknames: *Musiciolus*, *Faustus* (Lucky), *[U]rsus* (Bear), *Luxsuriu[s]* (Luxurious) and *Pascen[ti]us* (Grazing?).

The other scenes of the mosaic show an obscene dance: two nude men, in distorted positions, one with a dangling penis, both handling crossed rattlesticks like dwarves or pygmies in Roman Nile Flood mosaics, and Venus standing and holding a mirror in her raised right hand. She is nude, she covers her pubes with her left hand. A little Amor offers her a wreath. It has been suggested that Venus' place almost in front of the entrance to a back room would hint to the place where a client could buy and make love. The gesture of her left hand, however, argues against this interpretation.

32. The Temple of the Shipbuilders (Tempio dei *Fabri Navales*; III, ii, 2)

This guild temple, along the western *decumanus*, was built at the end of the 2nd century, on top of a workshop dating to ca AD 100. Behind and under the temple, at a far lower level, are the remains of a fuller's workshop (*fullonica*).

A statue base, in the left rear corner of the forecourt, bears the following text (*CIL* XIV 169; *AE* 1955, 177):

P(ublio) MARTIO QUI[R(ina)]
  PHILIPPO
CURATORI VIAE PRAE[NESTI]NAE
AEDILICIO CURULI V(iatori) Q(uaestori) A[B AER]ARIO
TRIBUNO FABRUM NAV[AVALIUM PORT]ENS(ium)
PLEBES CORPORIS [FABRUM NAVAL]IUM
OSTIENS(ium) QUI[BUS EX S(enatus) C(onsulto) COIRE LI]CET
PATRONO [OPTIM]O
      S(ua) P(ecunia) P(osuerunt)

For Publius Martius Philippus, from (the tribus*) Quirina, curator of the Praenestine Road,* aedilicius curulis *(assistant), (state) messenger, keeper of the treasury,* tribunus *(chief) of the shipbuilders at Portus, the ordinary members of the guild of the ship-builders placed (the statue), who by decree of the Senate had permission to have meetings, for their excellent patron, at their own expense have placed (the base and statue)*

The inscription dates to the reign of the emperor Septimius Severus. The Ostian shipbuilders (*fabri navales*) had a splendid, large guild-house (now called *Schola del Traiano*) on the opposite side of the street. It has an impressive semicircular entrance.

The sanctuary has a deep forecourt in the form of a peristyle, a temple in its axis, and a courtyard behind the temple. In the forecourt lie 47 columns of marble from Thasos. So this part of the sanctuary lost it religious function in late antiquity and became an open deposit. The columns are of the same type that has been used in the so-called Christian basilica, one of the next buildings along the *decumanus* (see no 33). Some columns mention the man who owned and traded in marble (*AE* 1945, 55b):

VOLUSIANI V(iri) C(larissimi)   *Of Volusianus, a very renowned man*

This Volusianus, evidently a Roman senator, has not been identified with certainty. Candidates are Caius Caeionius Rufus Volusianus Lampadius, prefect of the guard in AD 355 and prefect of Rome in AD 365-366 (see no 37), or his nephew, Rufius Antonius Agrypnius Volusianus, who was prefect of Rome in AD 417 and 418. As the former was pagan and the latter became Christian just before his death in AD 437, the second option is appealing. Augustine wrote him a letter in AD 412.

33. THE SO-CALLED CHRISTIAN BASILICA (CD 'BASILICA CRISTIANA'; III, i, 4)

This building, along the western *decumanus*, a 2nd century *domus* converted into two parallel, long porticoes ending up in a *nymphaeum* (fountain) and a *triclinium* (dining room), is dated to the end of the 4th or the beginning of the 5th century AD (*fig. 37*). On the architrave in the left portico, at the entrance to the *nymphaeum*, one finds the following inscription (*AE* 1967, 76):

IN XP *(Christo)* GEON FISON TIGRIS EUFRATA (and an incised branch)
TIGRI[N]IANORUM SUMITE FONTES (and an incised ivy leaf)

In Christ; Geon Fison Tigris Euphrates. Take (plural), i.e., drink from the sources of the Tigriniani

After the initial word In follows the *chrismon*, the combination of the Greek characters X (Ch) and P (R). See also no 22.

The function of the building is unclear. Suggestions include: a Christian church, school, library or hotel for pilgrims, or a *domus* of an aristocratic family, the Tigriniani. Whether some kind of association between the river Tiger and the Tigrianiani is intended, is not clear. The inscription mentions the four rivers of the earthly Paradise. There is a *nymphaeum* in the apse of the rear wall and there are rooms, perhaps for guests or pilgrims. The latter may have been invited to drink water offered by the family. Some doubts regarding the function of the building remain. Apart from the *nymphaeum* and the use of marble wall revetments it has nothing in common with the layout of other late aristocratic *domus*.

The idea that the four rivers of life have their source in Christ is also visible in a mosaic of the Basilica of Cosmas and Damianus (AD 527-530) in Rome. Christ is presented there as the divine lamb. Sedulius' *Carmen Paschale* (3.173-175), dated to AD 425, compares the four gospels to rivers: *Qualiter ex uno paradisi fonte leguntur quattuor ingentes procedere*

Fig. 37. The so-called Christian Basilica (photo author).

cursibus amnes, ex quibus in totum sparguntur flumina mundum (Like four enormous streams they are said to flow from one well of the paradise along their courses, from which rivers are distributed over the whole world).

The adjectival name Tigriniani is possibly derived from Tigrinus, a priest who restored buildings in and around Rome between ca AD 440 and 460. Tigrinus may have used Volusianus' columns. One of the columns on the right side of the right portico bears a careless inscription that reads (*AE* 1945, 55b):

VOLUSIANI V(iri) C(larissimi)   *Of Volusianus, a very renowned man*

This Roman senator may have been Rufius Antonius Agrypnius Volusianus, prefect of Rome in AD 417 and 418 who became a Christian just before his death in AD 437. Augustine wrote a letter to him in AD 412 (see no 32).

It is not impossible that Monica, mother of Augustine, who died in Ostia in AD 387 (Augustine, *Confessiones* 9.8-12), visited the building. She died in an apartment building with a garden from which the Tiber could be seen, perhaps the Building of Jupiter and Ganymedes (see no 15). A fragmentary inscription on a marble slab used as the cover of a terracotta sarcophagus, found in the necropolis to the east of Ostia (Borgo di Ostia), now in the Basilica of St. Aurea in modern Ostia, bears the *epitaphium Monicae*, epitaph in honour of Monica, perhaps written by Anicius Auchenius Bassus, who was consul in 408. The text can be restored thanks to copies in medieval manuscripts (*AE* 1948, 44):

HIC POSUIT CINE[RES GENITRIX CASTISSIMA PROLIS]
AUGUSTINE TU[I(s) ALTERA LUX MERITI(s)]
QUI SERVANS PA[CIS CAELESTIA IURA SACERDOS]
COMMISSOS PO[PULOS MORIBUS INSTITUTIS]
GLORIA VOS M[AIOR GESTORUM LAUDE CORONAT]
VIRTUTUM MA[TER FELICIOR SUBOLE]

Here she placed her ashes, the very chaste mother of her son
Augustine, second light of (to) your merit(s), you
who as priest guarding the heavenly laws of peace teaches
the peoples entrusted to you by good mores
A glory greater than martial deeds crowns you both
The mother of virtues (is) luckier by her son

According to D.R. Boin the mother of virtues is not Monica but the personification of Love.

34. THE SHOPS OF THE FISHMONGERS AND THE SO-CALLED MEAT MARKET (TABERNAE DEI PESCIVENDOLI E CD. MACELLUM; IV, v, 1-2)

The two shops (*tabernae*) of the fishmongers (*Macellum piscorium*), near the crossroads of the *decumanus* to the west of the *castrum*, is dated to the middle of the 3rd century AD. There are marble tables for the cutting of fish and a basin in which live fish was kept. Only part of the complex could be closed as is shown by a threshold with a groove. Behind the entrance is a black-and-white mosaic showing a dolphin with a squid in its jaws. The inscription near the entrance, which can be read from the inside of the shop, reads (*CIL* XIV S 4757; *fig. 38*):

INBIDE (= invide)	*Jealous man*
CALCO TE	*I trample upon you*

Between the words *calco* and *te* an ivy leaf is depicted. G. Becatti assumed that the scene might mean the cursing of dolphins as they would be rivals of fishermen. In antiquity, however, the dolphin was a people's and fishermen's friend. Squids, however, had a negative connotation. Therefore K.M.D. Dunbabin's interpretation that the fishmongers would like to crush

Fig. 38. Mosaic in the Shops of the Fishmongers (photo author).

an envious rival in the same manner that the dolphin consumes the squid is more convincing. Trampling is a very old metaphorical action, indicating subjection of an opponent by placing a foot on him. So the inscription has an apotropaic function, intending to ward off evil powers (see also no 35). The motif of a dolphin eating a squid is also present in mosaics of the Baths of the Seven Wise Men and *statio* 23 of the Square of the Guilds (see no 7); evidently it belonged to the repertoire of mosaicists. The theme *invidia* or Gr. *phthonos* (envy) is a frequent topic in Roman mosaics. In funerary inscriptions death is also described as jealous.

A black-and-white mosaic in a shop in the southern corner of the Terme dell'Invidioso (V, v, 1) depicts a successful fisherman and a boy with spread fingers who is called *inbidiosos* (see no 37).

Instead of *invide* and *invidiosus* the mosaicists have written *inbide* and *inbidiosos*. This shift from v to b (compare Venus > Benus) occurs more frequently in the 3rd century AD. As in Spanish the v is usually pronounced as b. The phenomenon also occurs in Greek inscriptions (e.g. Victor > Biktor).

Through a corridor between the two shops one arrives at an open space which was until recently assumed to be the (or a) Meat market (*macellum*). The presence of a podium supporting five columns is an unusual feature in meat markets. The central one has a vertical inscription (on the west side), which can probably be dated to the 4th century (Meiggs 1973, p. 399):

LEGE ET INTEL[LE]GE MUTU[M] LOQUI AD MACELLU[M]

*Read and understand that people are talking a lot (*mutu = multum*) at the meat market*
Or:
*Read and understand that a mute man (*mutu = mutum*) is talking at the meat market*

The first translation implies a warning against gossip at the market. The careful form of the inscription, however, discounts that such a banality is intended. According to Meiggs the words lege et intellege have a Christian flavour. Compare passages in the Bible, *Matthew* 24.15 and *Marcus* 13.14: ...*qui legit, intelligat* (that he who reads, may understand), *The Acts* 8.30: *putasne intelligis quae legis* (do you understand what you are reading?). I would add Augustine's *tolle lege* (pick up and read). The word *mutu(m)* may indicate that a miracle happened: a dumb man began to talk (compare *Lucas* 11.14). The column does not prove that the open space was a meat market (*macellum*) because it was found outside the square, reused in the *Nymphaeum* opposite the Fish-market, at the crossroads of the the *decumanus*, Via Epagathiana and Via della Foce (I, xiv, 1). The inscription was fashioned when the column was in a horizontal position.

The square of the so-called Macellum has a long history, from ca 90-60 BC until the 5th century AD.

According to an inscription on fragments of a marble table (*CIL* XIV S 4719) the Macellum was repaired by Aurelius Anicius Symmachus, prefect of Rome in AD 418-420 and member of a famous pagan, senatorial family. The fragments were found along the *decumanus*, between the Via dei Molini and the Forum as well as in the Via dei Molini. Other inscriptions mentioning a *macellum* or the very same one are *CIL* XIV 375 (see Appendix 3 and 4) and *CIL* XIV 423. So, the Macellum seems to have been situated somewhere along the *decumanus*. The enormous marble columns in front of the corridor between the fish shops may be an indication that the so-called Macellum was really a meat market.

35. THE HOUSE OF THE DESCENDING ZEUS
(DOMUS DEL GIOVE FULMINATORE; IV, iv, 3)

This old Republican atrium-house (*domus*), originally with a *peristylium* at the rear, built in the 2nd century BC, has an entrance (*fauces*, which means throat) with a black-and-white mosaic depicting an apotropaic phallus, intended to avert evil. The mosaic dates to the 2nd century AD. In the left rear part of the atrium is a little, marble altar with a Greek inscription (*SEG* 55, 1082):

ΔΙΙ   *To Descending Zeus*
KATA{I}
BATEI
(transcription: *Dii kataibatei*)

The epithet *kata(i)bates* should be interpreted as Zeus (Iupiter) coming down from heaven to throw thunderbolts. If the altar really belongs to the house, it was once struck by a thunderbolt. The altar was, however, found in the so-called Byzantine Baths (Terme bizantine; IV, iv, 8), which in the 4th century were built upon the peristyle at the rear of the house.

Interestingly, a second marble altar or base, found in situ, in the right-hand part of the atrium, but perhaps also transferred from elsewhere, bears

Fig. 39. Statue base in the House of the Descending Zeus (photo author).

a Greek inscription too (*SEG* 55, 1083). It is dated to the 2nd century AD. Unfortunately it is heavily mutilated. Visible are on the front: -]ΠΙΕΜΟ[---]/ ΕΞΟΧ[---]/ ΕΛΛΑΔΙΟΣΧΑΙ…Ν[---]/ΣΤΡΑΤΙΑ (*fig. 39*) and on the right side: ΠΑΛΙΝ. Transcription: *-piemo-, exoch-, helladioschai, -n, stratia*, and *palin*. *Exochos* means excellent, *Helladios* is a proper name or it consists of two words, *helladi hos*: 'for Greece. Who also (*kai*)…' *Stratia* is either a female proper name or it means *stratia* army or it is a plural neutral adjective: of the army; *palin* means again. The text may have been an epigram in hexameters, with words in one long and two short syllables (**Exo**chos; **Hel**ladi: -˘˘; -˘˘). In one Latin inscription two soldiers, a Marcus Antonius from Thrace and a namesake from Alexandria have the surname Exochus (*AE* 1947, 208). If the object is funerary, it was taken from a cemetery outside the city walls. The house was still in use in the 4th century AD.

36. THE HOUSE OF THE FISHES (DOMUS DEI PESCI; IV, iii, 3)

This beautiful, aristocratic house, a typical late antique domus, is dated to the last quarter of the 3rd century AD. It is an adaptation of a house from ca 240. Some walls have vertical series of *tubuli*, terracotta tubes, through which hot air ascended. The system was a predecessor of modern heating systems.

The central, square scene of a polychrome mosaic, dated to the 4th century, in the north, high vestibule depicts a unique scene: a chalice of white glass with a serpentine fish in or decorated on it, flanked by two diving fish (not visible on the black-and-white photo), rendered in porphyry on a green background. The margins are decorated with grey 'wolf's teeth' (*figs 40a-40b*). To those who left the house, the chalice was in the right position. To those who entered, it was upside down. In view of the fish some scholars, among whom Becatti, presume that the house belonged to a rich Christian family.

The half round water basin, partly overlapping a square one in the courtyard of the house, would have been a baptismal fount. A lost little marble slab showing an incised fish, the symbol by which a Christian could identify a religious brother or sister, was found in its rear wall. It should be remarked, however, that images of fishes are not unusual in water basins of pagan Roman houses.

Unfortunately, hard epigraphic proof of Christian religion in the *domus* is missing. But the mosaic seems to be allegorical. The square emblem may represent a piece of textile decorated with symbols.

Fish was not consumed during the Eucharist but a chalice was used. Christian catacomb paintings around AD 300 illustrating the miraculous multiplication of five loaves of bread and two fishes (*Matthew* 14, 13-21)

IN SITU INSCRIPTIONS 95

Fig. 40a. Mosaic in the House of the Fishes (photo author).

Fig. 40b. Mosaic in the House of the Fishes. Drawing (from G. Becatti 1949).

show banquets of men reclining on semicircular couches with baskets, loaves and fishes. Incidentally the guests use a cup, probably a wine cup. The scenes may have more than one meaning. They refer to funerary meals and banquets in the afterlife, but they also remind us of the Last Supper (Eucharist). Though loaves are absent on the mosaic, the combination of a chalice and fish very likely points to Christian symbolism. A fifth century mosaic in a church at Tabgha, on the north side of the Sea of Galilea, depicts a basket with loaves flanked by two fish. In addition, a mosaic in the fifth century church Sant'Apollinare at Ravenna and a codex (6th century AD) show the Last Supper with two fish on a plate surrounded by seven pyramidal loaves, but no cups. The latter scenes differ from the description of the Last Supper in the New Testament which mentions only bread and wine. It seems that Christian symbols were interchangeable. The chalice on the mosaic may hint at the wine chalice of the Last Supper.

Another option is that the picture hints at baptismal regeneration. The church father Tertullian (*On baptism*, 1) writes: 'we, being the little fish, as Jesus Christ is our great fish, begin our life in the water and only while we abide in the water we are safe.' In addition, Roman funerary inscriptions define the fish as *ichthys zonton* in Greek (the fish of the living people).

The not too explicit symbolic mosaic may be explained by the fact that the Christian and pagan religions coexisted between 313 and 394. The house-owner may have taken into account the sensibility of pagans. An important argument is that usually mosaics in vestibules face the street side, which is not the case here. In addition, the vestibule is 45 cm above street level which means that it could only be entered via wooden stairs which could be removed.

The final option that the fish would refer to the job of the house owner may be ruled out as fishmongers did not keep fish in a chalice. In addition, it is highly unlikely that rich people were directly involved in the selling of fish.

Although the images may be crypto-Christian, some pagan elements have been found in or near the courtyard: a little statue of a Fortuna with a cornucopia and a very small marble round altar. In addition, the black-and-white mosaic in the reception hall features two diving fish flanking a trident, the attribute of Neptune, in one of the 42 panels. The elements, however, may be of an earlier date.

From ca AD 250 onward gravestones were reused in floors. Scarcity of materials may have been the cause. Twenty-five fragments were found in this house. In the floor of the square fountain with a small marble pyramid used as spout is an inserted plaster copy of a recycled, complete, funerary marble slab with this inscription (Becatti 1948; *fig. 41*):

D(is) M(anibus)
PRIMUS FECIT
CONIUGI BENEME
RENTI KALAEEMERE
   UNI
LOC(us) SIBI CONC(essus) A MUN(atia) IUSTA

To the Spirits of the Dead. Primus made (this) for his wife Kala(h)emera, well deserving it. Uni. The place was conceded to him by Munatia Justa

The initial abbreviation DM (*Dis Manibus*, dative of *Di Manes*) is extremely frequent in Roman funerary inscriptions. In Greek inscriptions the *di manes* are called *theoi katachthonioi*, gods of the underworld. Bodies were mortal but souls were held to be immortal. *Fecit* means: made, or: had (it) made. The causative form is usually the best translation. The meaning of the word *uni* (written in lowercase letters) is not clear. If it belongs to *locus*, the exceptional word *unilocus* would mean one (and the same) place. Evidently, Primus' wife was of Greek origin. Her name means 'Nice Day' (compare New Greek: *kalimēra*). Instead of the genitive on *-ae* the

Fig. 41. Inscription the House of the Fishes. Copy (photo author).

scribe wrote *-e*. Primus and his wife may have been slaves of a lady with the name Munatia Justa. Other reused gravestones are present in the Baths of Mithras, in late antique *domus*, in one of the Shops of the Fishmongers, and in the Synagogue, in the southwest corner of the excavation site.

37. THE CAMPUS OF THE GREAT MOTHER
(CAMPO DELLA *MAGNA MATER*; IV, i)

This triangular sanctuary, bordered on the south side by the Ciceronian city wall, contains a large temple with side-niches dedicated to Cybele, *Magna Mater Deum* ('the Great Mother of the Gods'), a chapel dedicated to her beloved shepherd Attis, a small temple dedicated to Bellona, goddess of war, and a guild-hall (*schola*) of the *Dendrophori*, tree-bearers of Cybele.

According to the Calendar of Philocalus from AD 354 the festivities took place in March:

15 March: idibus cannus intrat (on the Ides reed enters). Reed was transported to Cybele's temple by the *cannophori* ('reed carriers'). The rite may have commemorated the reed of the river Gallos in which the newborn Attis was placed as a foundling.

22 March: arbor intrat (the tree comes in). This rite refers to the transformation of the dying Attis into a pine tree.

24 March: sanguem or sanguis (blood (day)). This was the main day of mourning for Attis. It was bloody as priests wounded, or even castrated themselves (see below).

25 March: Hilaria (feast of joy). On this day the 'resurrection' of Attis as a pine tree was commemorated.

26 March: requietio (repose). This was a rest day without activities.

27 March: lavatio (washing). On this final feast day the statue of Cybele was washed, in Ostia probably in the sea. It may have been an act of purification.

Attis' chapel dates to the Julio-Claudian (with additions in later centuries), Cybele's temple to the Antonine period. Her cult, however, was already introduced into Rome at the crucial end of the second Punic War, in 204 BC. The ship carrying her black stone from Pessinus in Asia Minor to Rome ran aground in the Tiber near Ostia, but was set afloat by a woman, Claudia Quinta, who could by so-doing prove her chastity (Ovid, *Fasti* 4.291-328). Originally Cybele was an Anatolian fertility goddess, called Kubaba in Hittite.

In the southeast corner of the terrain, at the far end of the *porticus*, is the *fossa sanguinis* (the pit of blood). A bull used to be slaughtered above a wooden plank-bridge with holes. Whoever was to be initiated, stood under it and was sprinkled and in this way baptized with blood (*tauroboliatus*). In so-doing, the strength of the bull was transferred to the initiate. It was a kind of rebirth.

The entrance to the chapel of Attis is flanked by Panes (plural of Pan), wild demi-gods with goats' feet. The plaster copy of a marble statue representing the recumbent semi-nude Attis with a radiate crown, shepherd's staff (*pedum*), fruit, the sickle used for the castration at his feet, and a separated penis (original now in the Vatican Museums, dated to ca AD 150) bears the following inscription (*CIL* XIV 38):

NUMINI ATTIS C(aius) CARTILIUS EUPLUS
EX MONITU DEAE

*To the divine power of Attis Gaius Cartilius Euplus
by a warning of the goddess*

Cartilius was a freedman (*libertus*), as the surname Euplus derives from Gr. *euplous* (good sea trip); the goddess, who warned him, probably in a dream, was Cybele. The same man offered seven other statues with a similar inscription. They are in the local museum. Particularly interesting is a Dionysus statue from the 1st century AD, reused and given by a Volusianus (*tauroboliatus*), probably Caius Ceionius Rufus Volusianus Lampadius, the anti-Christian prefect of Rome between AD 365 and 390 (*AE* 1955, 180).

According to the myth Attis emasculated himself after an affair under a pine tree. He died and was transformed into the pine tree. It symbolizes a kind of resurrection. Priests of Cybele used to imitate Attis' cruel act and were called *galli* (plur. of *gallus*: cock). The reason may be that Attis' story took place near the river Gallos. The leader of the *galli* was called *archigallus*.

The *Hastiferi* (Lance-bearers) played a role in the cult of Bellona, occasionally performing war dances, probably linked to the Cybele cult.

In front of the Cybele temple stands a 2 m high (!) statue base with inscriptions (*CIL* XIV 325), destined for two statues. On the upper plinth we read:

---] III KA[L(endas)]
[L(ucio) SE]PTIMIO SEVERO PERTINACE AUG(usto) II
[CLODIO SEPTIMIO ALBINO CAES(are)] CO(n)S(ulibus)

---] on the third day before the Kalendae....
when L. Septimius Severus Pertinax Augustus II (and) Clodius Septimius Albinus Caesar were consuls

Their names allow the inscription to be dated to AD 194.
On the lower right part of the front only this fragmentary text is visible:

---[DIE]S III KALE[NDAS]
---[P(ublii)] CLAU[D(ii)] VERA[TI ABASCANTIANI]
---[S]UMM(as) DIES VIII [I]DU[S I]ANUAR(ias)
---[DIES SUPRA S]CRIPTOS NON OBSERVAVERIT
…SUMMAS S(upra) S(criptas) REI PUBLIC(ae) [OST(iensis)?]
…REFUNDI SIC FACTUS EST

[On the birthday?] of P. Claudius Abascantianus, the eighth day before the Ides of January (6 January) sums of money [have to be paid]. Whoever does not respect the birthdays mentioned above is forced to refund in this way the sums of money mentioned above to the city of Ostia

On the left side we read:

[M(arcus) ANTIUS CRESCE]NS CALPURNIANUS V(ir) C(larissimus)
[PONTIF(ex) VOLKANI] ET AEDIUM SACR(arum)
[SI FIAT SINE VE]XATIONE ULLIUS STATUAE
[ANTE POSITAE UT]RAMQUE STATUAM IN
[INSCRIPTIONE INS]CRIBT(am) CONSTITUERE
[PERMITTO D(omino)] N(ostro) IMP(eratore) SEPTIMIO AUG(usto) II
                CO(n)S(ule)

Marcus Antius Crescens Calpurnianus, a very renowned man,
high priest of Volkanus and the sacred buildings
If it can happen without damage of any statue
which was placed earlier, [I permit] that both statues
mentioned in the inscription are placed
when Our Lord Emperor Septimius Augustus II was consul

This text refers to two statues, evidently one for Publius Abascantianus, and probably the other for his brother Horatius Abascantianus, in AD 194.
A marble tablet (*CIL* XIV 326) mentions the birthdays of Publius Abascantianus and many others in chronological order, listing the individual fi-

nancial contributions to the collective *dies natalis* festivities. The tablet was made by Publius' father P. Claudius Abascantus, *III Provinciarum libertus* (freedman of the Three Provinces (of Gaul)). This implies that he made a successful career for himself in Ostia after having been a slave (*servus publicus*) of the Three Galliae (compare *CIL* XIV 327: *trium Galliarum*). His name is mentioned in an *album* (list) of the *corpus dendrophorum*: he was twice *QQ* (*quinquennalis*), president for five years of the Guild of the Tree-bearers. He lost his wife, Modestia Epigone (a freedwoman) in Ostia on 23 June 177 (*CIL* XIV 328) and a foster-son (*alumnus*) at the age of 8 years, 5 months and 18 days (*CIL* XIV 327). The latter was buried in a marble sarcophagus depicting two sea centaurs holding up the inscription (now in Museo Torlonia at Rome).

The front of a base, which originally stood in front of the temple (now in the local museum), mentions another son of Abascantus (*CIL* XIV 324):

P(ublio) CL(audio) P(ubli) F(ilio) HORAT(io)
ABASCANTIANO (the characters NT are combined in a ligature)
FIL(io) DULCISSI
MO P(ublius) CL(audius)
ABASCANTUS
⎯⎯ PATER
Q̄Q̄ IĪ CORP(oris) DENDRO
PHORUM OSTIENS(ium)

For Publius Claudius, son of Publius, Horatius
Abascantianus, his very lovely son,
Publius Claudius
Abascantus, his father,
president for 5 years, for the second time, of the Guild of the Tree-
bearers of Ostia (placed the base and statue)

On the right side:

C(aius) ANTIUS CRESCENS CALPUR
NIANUS PONT(ifex) VOLK(ani)
ET AEDIUM SACR(arum) STATU
AM PONI IN CAMPO MATRIS
DEUM INFANTILEM PERMISI
    VIIII KAL(endas) APRIL(es)
[[Plautiano]] ĪI ET GETA II CO(n)S(ulibus)

*Gaius Antius Crescens Calpurnius, high priest of Volkanus
and of the sacred buildings: I have permitted that the statue of the child
was placed in the Campus of Mater Deum (Mother of the Gods)
on the eighth day before the first day of April
when [Plautianus] II and Geta II were consuls*

The text is dated 25 March AD 203.

More than thirty objects with inscriptions, found on the Campus, are now in the local museum and its stores (see A.-K. Rieger, *Heiligtümer in Ostia*). Those that can be dated precisely range in date from AD 143 until 256.

38. The Pavement of the Boundary Stones (*Semita* dei Cippi; V, i)

Two travertine boundary stones with a curved upper end, standing a short distance apart, on the border between street and pavement, both carry the following inscription (Bakker 1994, p. 197; *fig. 42*):

HAEC	*This is*
SEMITA HOR(reorum)	*the pavement of a*
P R I	*private (?) storehouse*
EST	

There is no consensus regarding the interpretation of the characters P R I. It has been suggested that R and I may refer to *Regio* I, because Ostia was divided in five *regiones*. Which parts of the city fell under each region is unknown. The current numbering of five *regiones* is modern. The P can hardly mean *principium* (beginning) as the stones do not stand at the beginning of the street. Probably P R I is an abbreviated adjective: *privatorum* (private), if it depends on *horreorum*. Another possible meaning may be: *populi Romani iussu* or *iuris* (by decree of or belonging to the jurisdiction of the Roman people). In the latter case the inscriptions would date to the Republican period. *Semita* can mean street, path and pavement, in this case probably the latter. The stones stand right in front of a storehouse (*horrea*).

A boundary stone of lava in Pompeii, also with a curved upper side, found next to the Fortuna Augusta temple, near the Forum, bears this inscription (*CIL* X 821):

M(arci) TULLI M(arci) F(ilii)

Fig. 42. Boundary stone along the Semita dei cippi (photo author).

AREA PRIVATA

Private domain of Marcus Tullius, son of Marcus

The stone belonged to the domain of the *gens Tullia* (*Regio* VII, iv, 3-7). This comparison suggests that the *semita* in Ostia means the pavement rather than the street in front of a store. Few rooms of the store itself have been preserved.

39. THE SHOP OF THE JEALOUS MAN (TERME DELL'INVIDIOSO; V, v, 2)

A black-and-white mosaic in the shop in the south corner of the Baths of the Jealous Man depicts a fisherman standing in his ship, holding two fish in his right hand. A boy holding his fingers spread in the direction of the successful fisherman is labelled (Becatti 1961, p. 219):

INBIDIOSOS *The jealous man*

The boy being called jealous makes an apotropaic gesture. The fisher, seen at a 90-degree angle, does the same. Their emotional behaviour may point to fierce competition, probably due to scarcity of fish. The mosaic is dated to around AD 200-250. The basin in the centre of the floor may have held fish (see no 34). For another illustration of jealousy see no 33. The scribe wrote *inbidiosos* instead of *invidiosos*, showing the shift from v to b in the 3rd century. The letter b could likewise change into v (e.g. *habitavit* > *avitavit*).

40. THE MITHRAEUM OF FELICISSIMUS (MITREO DI FELICISSIMO; V, ix, 1)

The *Mithraeum* is dated to the middle of the 3rd century AD. The original entrance is on the north side. It could only be entered through an adjacent room for reasons of secrecy. The black-and-white mosaic near the entrance depicts the opening of a pit (for the remains of consumed animals), a metal bucket, the caps of the Dioscuri (who personify the cycle of life and death) and a burning altar, which faces the entrance. Over its entire length the mosaic displays the symbols of the seven grades into which followers of Mithras could be successively initiated. On top is this text (*AE* 1946, 118; *figs 43-44*):

FELICISSIMUS
EX VOTO F(ecit)

Felicissimus has made (the mosaic) because of a vow

Under the inscription a crater between twigs is visible. The seven grades of initiation with their symbols, from the bottom up in ascending hierarchical order, are illustrated in panels which resemble a ladder:

Corax/corvus (raven):	crow, cup, herald staff (related to the planet Hermes/Mercurius)
Nymphus (male bride):	diadem, lamp, (missing symbol) (to Aphrodite/Venus)
(or: *Cryphius* (hidden man))	
Miles (soldier):	lance, helmet, soldier's dress (to Ares/Mars)
Leo (lion):	thunderbolt, *sistrum* (Isis-rattle), fire-shovel (to Zeus/Jupiter)
Perses (Persian):	moon sickle, scythe, star (to Selene/Luna/Moon)
Heliodromus (sun-runner):	whip, crown, torch (to Helios/Sol/Sun)

Fig. 43. Mosaic in the Mithraeum of Felicissimus, detail (photo author).

Pater (father): sickle, cap, staff, bowl (to Kronos/Saturnus)

The seven grades are associated with the seven planets. The same hierarchical sequence is found in inscriptions from the *Mithraeum* under the Santa Prisca in Rome. The rites or festivities were called: *hierocoracia, cryfii* (?), unknown, *leontica, persica, heliaca* and *patrica* (*CIL* VI 749-753).

Mithraea (*spelaea* (caves)) were images of the cosmos (see below). Cosmic and astrological aspects of Mithraic religion are also visible in many reliefs which have found in the rear sections of *Mithraea* along the *limes*, the boundary of the Roman Empire along the Rhine and Danube. Mithras, born from a rock with wheat ears in his hands, is shown hunting and killing the bull, with his head turned, listening to the message of the Sun, brought by a crow. The killing takes place during the transition from light to darkness. The Sun is on the left, the Moon in the upper right-hand corner. To the left stands Cautes with raised torch, to the right Cautopates with hanging torch. Sometimes personifications of seasons or winds are visible in the corners. A dog and a snake lick the blood of the bull, a scorpion tackles his genitals and a wheat ear springs from his tail. Sometimes a crater and a lion are rendered under the bull. After the killing Mithras dines with the Sun, a rite that was imitated by the initiated. In many inscriptions Mithras is called Sol Invictus (the Unconquered Sun). According to R. Beck (2006) nine elements in the bull-killing scenes point to con-

Fig. 44. Mosaic in the Mithraeum of Felicissimus, detail (photo author).

stellations of the heavens: the bull would be *Taurus*, Cautes and Cautopates *Gemini*, the Dog *Canis Minor* or *Maior*, the snake *Hydra*, the lion *Leo*, the crater *Crater*, the wheat ear *Spica*, the raven *Corvus*, the scorpion *Scorpio*. Mithras would travel along these constellations during a solar eclipse 'when the Sun was in Leo'. Mithraic religion would also imply the descending of the soul to earth and its returning to heaven. The seven grades symbolize the ascension to heaven along the seven planets. Beck bases his theory on *De antro nympharum* (*On the cave of the nymphs*) 6 of the Neo-platonist philosopher Porphyry (ca AD 250):

> 'Similarly, the Persians call the place a cave where they introduce an initiate to the mysteries, revealing to him the path by which the souls descend (*kathodos*) and go back again (*exodos*). For Euboulos tells us that Zoroaster was the first to dedicate a natural cave in honour of Mithras, the creator and father of all; it was located in the mountains near Persia and had flowers and springs. This cave bore for him the image of the cosmos which Mithras had

created, and the things which the cave contained, by their proportionate arrangement, provided him with symbols of the elements and climates of the cosmos.'

In chapter 24 we read:

'As a creator and lord of genesis Mithras is placed in the region of the celestial equator with the north to his right and the south to his left; to the south, because of its heat, they assigned Cautes and to the north <Cautopates> because of the coldness of the north wind' (Translations from: *Porhyry. The Cave of the Nymphs in the Odyssey*, edited & translated by J. Duffy, P. Sheridan, L.G. Westerink, and J. White. Buffalo: Arethusa 1969).

About the initiation rites there is little information, and what there is is probably biased, provided by Christian writers. According to Firmicus Maternus (*De errore profanarum religionum* 19; ca AD 346) the *nymphus* (male bride, veiled, with a lamp) greeted: '[See] *nymphus*, hail *nymphus*, hail new light!' According to Tertullian the *miles* received a mark on his forehead. They offered him a wreath on the point of a sword and placed it on his head. Then he had to cast it off with his hand saying that Mithras is his wreath. According to Porphyry (ch. 15) *leones* got honey instead of water for washing their hands. Probably the golden colour of honey symbolized fire, enemy of water, and the rite was a symbolic fire-baptism. According to the same author (ch. 16) *Perses* also received honey, since he was the keeper of fruits. Honey had preservative power.

41. THE GRANARY OF HORTENSIUS (HORREA DI ORTENSIO; V, xii, 1)

The grain store to the south of the *decumanus* lies ca 1 metre below street level. It is one of the oldest *horrea* in Ostia, usually dated to the Julio-Claudian but according to recent research should be dated to the late Republican period.

In the northwest corner is a shrine with a polychrome floor mosaic (*fig. 45*), dated to the second half of the 3rd century AD. Its inscription reads (Becatti 1961, p. 231):

L(ucius) HORTE[N]SIUS HERACLIDA N(avarchus) CL(assis) PR(aetoriae) MIS(enensis) EX VOTO /
TEMPLUM FECIT IULIUS VICTORINUS SACER(dos) TESSEL(avit)

Lucius Horte(n)sius Heraclida, captain of the praetorian fleet at Misenum, has the temple made because of a vow; Julius Victorinus, priest, has the mosaic made

The fleet commander founded a chapel in this granary, possibly because of his escorting the grain fleet. The floor mosaic of *opus sectile* (cut work) shows a green marble disk with flames covering three arms of a cross, flanked by torches. The disk may represent the Sun, possibly assimilated with Serapis. A bilingual inscription from Ostia mentions Helios Megalos Serapis (*CIL* XIV 47). Many shippers of the military fleet, which had its base at Misenum, in the bay of Naples, originated from Egypt. The Greek cognomen Heraclida shows that Lucius was a freedman. Obviously, Julius Victorinus did not make the mosaic himself as his religious function does not seem to be compatible with laying mosaics. Thus he financed it.

On a plaster cast of a very small marble altar or base, now standing on the podium in front of the rear wall, we find the following text with the name of the same donor (*AE* 1953, 262; *fig. 45*):

L(ucius) HORT
ENSIUS
HERAC
LIDA N(avarchus)
FECIT

Lucius Hortensius Heraclida, captain, has (this) made

Fig. 45. Mosaic in the Shrine of Hortensius (photo author).

42. The Cemetery of Via Ostiensis

The cemetery outside the Ciceronian city walls, in front of the Porta Romana, has many tombs to the south of the Via Ostiensis. They belonged to members of the higher social class: knights (*equites*), magistrates (*duumviri, aediles, decuriones*) and priests (*Augustales*). The other necropolis, outside Porta Laurentina, was destined for freedmen (*liberti*) and slaves (*servi, vernae*). Until the reign of Hadrian cremation was practised, later on inhumation gradually became the trend. Ashes were put in *ollae* (pots) or urns. These were placed in *columbaria* (dovetill niches in the walls of a funerary chamber). Bodies were buried in sarcophagi which were placed in *arcosolia*, large semicircular niches. The necropolis was used from the 1st century BC until the 3rd century AD.

One of the most impressive monuments is the square Tomb of Hermogenes, originally revetted with marble, very near Porta Romana (along the south side of the Via Ostiensis).

42.1. The Tomb of Hermogenes

The inscription on the marble slab on the street side reads (*CIL* XIV S 4642; *fig. 46*):

C(aio) DOMITIO L(uci) FIL(io) PAL(atina) F[ABIO]
          HERMOGENI
E[QUITI] ROMANO SCRIBAE AEDIL(um) CURUL(ium) DEC(urioni) ADLE[CT(o)] /
FL[AM(ini) DIVI H]AD[RIA]NI IN CUIUS SACERDOTIO SOLUS AC PRIMUS LUD[OS /
SCAENIC]OS SUA P[E]CUNIA FECIT AEDILI HUNC SPLENDIDISSIMUS ORDO DECUR[ION(um) /
FUN(ere) PUBL]ICO HON[O]RAVIT EIQUE STATUAM EQUESTREM SUBSCRIPTIONE OB AMOR[EM /
ET INDUSTR]IAM O[MNE]M IN FORO PONENDAM PECUNIA PUBLICA DECRE[V]I[T /
INQUE L]OC[UM E]IUS [AE]DIL(em) SUBSTITUENDUM NON PUTAVIT IN SOLACIUM FAB[I PAT]RIS /
[QU]I OB HONORES [EI H]A[BI]T[O]S HS L̄ M̄(ilia) N̄(ummum) REI PUBLICAE DEDIT EX QUORUM USURIS QUINCUN[CI]BUS /
[Q]UOD ANNIS XIII K[AL(endas)] AUG(ustas) DIE NATALI EIUS DECURIONIB(us) DL PRAESENTIB(us) IN FORO ANT[E] STAT(uam)

S(upra)] S(criptam) /
[DIVI]DANTUR [ET] DECURIALIBUS SCRIBIS CERARIS XXXVII
S LIBRARIS XII S ITEM LICTORIBUS [XXV]   L(ucius) FABIUS
SP(uri)   F(ilius)   EUTYCHUS   LICTOR   CURIATIUS   SCRIB[A]
CER[ARIUS] /
ET LIBRARIUS Q̄(uin)Q̄(uennalis) COLLEGI(i) FABR(um) [TIG]NUAR
(iorum) OSTIENS(ium) ET ARTORIA EIUS PAR[ENTES]

For Gaius Domitius Fabius Hermogenes, son of Lucius, from (the tribus) Palatina, Roman knight, secretary of the curulian aediles, co-opted town councillor, priest (flamen) of the deified Hadrian during which priesthood he, alone and first, organized theatrical plays at his own expense, aedilis. *The very illustrious class of the town councillors has honoured him with a public funeral. And this (class) has decided that an equestrian statue had to be placed on the Forum for him with the inscription 'because of his love and total dedication', at public expense; and it has not been considered to appoint an* aedilis *in his place as consolation for his father Fabius, who, in view of the honours bestowed on him (Gaius), has donated 50.000* sestertii *to the city; let each year, on his birthday, 13 days before the first day of August (19 July) from the interest of five twelfth be distributed 550* denarii *to the members of the town council, in their presence in front of the statue mentioned above on the forum, and to the members of the guild of the scribes of wax tablets 37.5* denarii, *to the copyists 12.5* denarii, *to the* lictores *25 (?)* denarii. *Lucius Fabius Eutychus, son of Spurius,* lictor *of assemblies (or public rites), scribe of wax tablets, copyist, president for five years of the builders' guild of Ostia, and Artoria, his parents.*

The inscription on the architrave, in two fragments now placed on the lower edge of the tomb, on the Porta Romana side and at the rear, reads (*CIL* XIV S 4643):

[---] C(aio)] DOMITIO L(uci) F(ilio) FABIO HER[MOGENI ---]
[---] DECURIO G]RATUITUS

[---] For Gaius Domitius Fabius Hermogenes, son of Lucius
[---] town councillor who did not (have to) pay an entrance-fee

This man probably died at the end of the 2nd century AD because a fragment of an Achilles sarcophagus found in his tomb dates to this time. Perhaps Domitius served as a priest in the Temple on the Square of the Guilds behind the Theatre. He was of local origin. His natural father, Lucius, a rich freedman, who eventually held a top function as president of one of the most powerful guilds, may have pushed him up the local social ladder. Gaius had a job in Rome: scribe of the curulian *aediles*, who were high magistrates of the state, overseers of the public order, markets and games. Gaius died young, during his *aedilis*-ship, when his parents were still alive. A base with his equestrian statue originally stood on the Forum (see no 16). As for the value of the gifts to officials: a *denarius* is a silver coin weighing circa four grams. The value of one *denarius* was 4 *sestertii*. The generosity of Domitius can be deduced by the fact that a legion soldier in the first centuries AD earned a minimum wage of 225 *denarii* per year.

Fig. 46. Inscription on the Mausoleum of C. Domitius Fabius Hermogenes (photo author).

The inscription on the base which carried Hermogenes' equestrian statue on the Forum (*CIL* XIV 353) tells us that the town council, meeting in the Temple of Roma and Augustus, took the decision to distribute *sportulae* (baskets with money) on the Forum on the occasion of Hermogenes' birthday.

At the north side of the parallel southern graveyard street is a base of travertine. Its text reads (*CIL* XIV S 4287; *fig. 47*):

HERCULI
HERMOGENIANO
SACRUM

Dedicated to Hercules Hermogenianus

So Hermogenes probably had his own private, tutelary deity. Another family, the Turranii, worshipped their Hercules Turranianus.

42.2. A tomb-door with inscription

Parallel to and to the south of the Via Ostiensis is a second street in the cemetery (the Via dei Sepolcri), bordered to the north by graves with *columbaria*. Some contain *ustrina* (funeral pyres). Halfway the street there is, at a lower level, behind a vestibule a monumental gate which gives access to the Tomb of the Little Arches (Tomba degli Archetti), a *columbarium*, which dates to the Claudian period. The anterior space was built in the second century AD. Originally it featured a mosaic showing an anchor and rostrum (stem). So the deceased may have been engaged in the sea trade. On the lintel of the travertine gate we read HMSN (*fig. 48*):

H(oc) M(onumentum) H(eredem) N(on) S(equitur)

This monument does not follow the heir

This means that, once the tomb remained property of the family, it could not be transferred to a heir.

42.3. A sarcophagus

A monumental marble sarcophagus, 2.37 m long and 1.90 m high, dated to ca AD 250, standing on a high travertine base along the south side of the street bears the following inscription (*CIL* XIV 314):

D(is) M(anibus)
SEX(to) CARMINIO PARTHENOPEO
EQ(uiti) R(omano) DEC(urioni) COL(oniae) OST(iensis) Q(uin)Q(uennali)
COLLEG(ii)
FABR(um) TIGNUARIOR(um) OST(iensium) ET

Fig. 47. Altar for Hercules Hermogenianus (photo author).

Fig. 48. Tomb of the Little Arches (photo author).

CARMINIAE BRISEIDI CONIUG(i) EIUS
SEX(tus) CARMINIUS PLOTINIANUS
FRATRI B̄(ene) M̄ (erenti)
IN FRONT(e) PED(es) XII IN AGR(o) PED(es) XXXV

To the Spirits of the Dead. For Sextus Carminius Parthenopeus, Roman knight, councillor of the colonia *Ostia, president for five years of the guild of the builders of Ostia, and for Carminia Briseïs, his wife. Sextus Carminius Plotinianus (gave the tomb and sarcophagus) to his brother as he deserved it. At the front twelve feet, in the field thirty-five feet*

Judging by the Greek *cognomina* Parthenopeus and Briseis, the deceased were a freedman and freedwoman. Their common patron was probably a member of the powerful family of the Sextii Carminii in Rome. Sextus' functions show that he had a splendid career both in Rome and in Ostia since the guild of the builders was Ostia's largest *collegium*. The measurements in Roman feet (29.8 cm, but in practice often 30 cm) refer to the width at the front and the length in the field of the tomb in which the sarcophagus originally stood or was to be placed.

APPENDIX 1

EPIGRAPHIC ABBREVIATIONS

AUG	Augustus (common title of Roman emperors)
BF	*beneficarius* (privileged soldier)
BM	*bene merens* (well-deserving)
C	Caius (pronounced as Gaius)
CAES	Caesar (common title of Roman emperors)
CL	*classis* (fleet)
COH	*cohors* (cohort)
COL	*colonia*
COS	*consulibus* (when …. were consuls)
D D	*decreto decurionum* (by decree of the town councillors)
D D	*donum* or *dono dedit* (he has given (it) as gift)
D M	*dis manibus* (to the *Di Manes*, Spirits of the Dead)
D S P F C	*de sua pecunia faciendam curavit/curaverunt* (with his own money, i.e. at his/their own expense he has/they had (it) made)
EEMM VV	*viri eminentissimi* (honorary title of the *praefecti praetorio*)
F	*filius* (son)
F C	*faciendum curavit/curaverunt* (he/they had it made)
FIL	*filius* (son)
H M H N S	*hoc monumentum heredem non sequitur* or *sequetur* (this monument will not follow the heir; in other words the heir is not allowed to use the tomb)
IMP	*imperator* (emperor)
IN AGR	*in agro* (in the field (in length))
IN FRONT	*in fronte* (at the front (in width))
L	Lucius
LIB	*libertus* (freedman); *liberta* (freedwoman)
M	Marcus
N	*navarchus* (captain of a ship)
N	*nepos* (grandson)
OST	*Ostiensis* (adjective of Ostia; Ostian; inhabitant of Ostia)
P	*pes* (Roman foot)
P	Publius

PED	*pedes* (Roman feet)
PONT MAX	*pontifex maximus* (high priest)
P P	*pater patriae* (father of the fatherland)
PR	*praetor*
PR URB	*praetor urbanus* (chief of the city (Rome))
PRAEF	*praefectus* (chief)
PRAEF ANN	*praefectus annonae* (chief of the grain supply)
Q	*quaestor* (financial official)
QQ	(*magister*) *quinquennalis* (president for five years, usually of a guild)
S	*semis* (half (0.5))
SACER	*sacerdos* (priest)
S C	*senatus consultum* (decree of the Senate of Rome)
S S	*supra script-* (written/mentioned above)
SEX	Sextus
TI	Tiberius
TRIB	*tribus* (subdivision of the Roman citizen body; Ostia belonged to the *tribus* Voturia and the *tribus* Palatina).
TRIB POT	*tribunicia potestate* (with the power of a *tribunus plebis*)
VC	*vir clarissimus* (a very renowned man; honorary title of a member of the Senate of Rome)
VIG	*vigiles* (watchmen; firemen)
VP	*vir perfectissimus* (a very perfect man; honorary title; originally for members of the *ordo* (class) of the *equites* (knights))
V S L M	*votum solvit libens merito* (he fulfilled his vow willingly and deservedly)

APPENDIX 2

THE REIGNS OF ROMAN EMPERORS

	Julio-Claudian dynasty	
	Augustus	31 BC-AD 14
	Tiberius	14-37
	Caligula	37-41
	Claudius	41-54
	Nero	54-68
Galba		68-69
Otho		69
Vitellius		69
	Flavian dynasty	
	Vespasian	69-79
	Titus	79-81
	Domitian	81-96
Nerva		96-98
Trajan		98-117
Hadrian		117-138
	Antonine dynasty	
	Antoninus Pius	138-161
	Marcus Aurelius	161-180
	Commodus	180-192
Pertinax		193
	Severan dynasty	
	Septimius Severus	193-211
	Caracalla	211-217
	Heliogabalus	218-222
	Severus Alexander	222-235

Maximinus Thrax	235-238
Gordian III	238-244
Philippus Arabs	244-249
Decius	249-251
Trebonianus Gallus	251-53
Valerianus	253-260
Gallienus	260-268
Claudius Gothicus	268-270
Aurelianus	270-275
Probus	276-282
Carus, Numerianus and Carinus	282-284
Diocletian	284-305
Tetrarchy	293-305
Maxentius	306-312
Constantinus (Constantine the Great)	312-337
Other emperors	337-391
Eugenius	392-394
Theodosius	379-395
Honorius and Theodosius iunior	408-423

APPENDIX 3

THE INSCRIPTION IN HONOR OF P. LUCILIUS GAMALA 'SENIOR'

The inscription in honour of P. Lucilius Gamala 'senior' (ca 80-30 BC). *CIL* XIV 375; Meiggs 1972, 558 no 1 From Portus (probably reused there); lost; known from a drawing by Pirro Ligorio (ca 1510-1583); the marble pilaster ('four feet high') had a slender form similar to that of *CIL* XIV 376 (see Appendix 4; the two pilasters may once have formed a pair or stood together in Ostia):

P(ublio) Lucilio / P(ublii) f(ilio) P(ublii) n(epoti) P(ublii) pro/nep(oti) Gamalae / aed(ili) sacr(is) Volk(ani) / aedili d(ecurionum) d(ecreto) allecto / gratis decurioni / pontifici
IIvir(o) censo/riae pot(estatis) quinquennal(i) / in comitis facto cura/tori pecuniae publicae exigen/dae et adtribuendae / in ludos cum accepisset public(e) / lucar remisit et de suo erogati/onem fecit / idem sua pecunia viam silice stravit / quae est iuncta foro ab arcu ad arcum / idem epulum trichilinis CCXVII / colonis dedit / idem prandium sua pecunia colonis / Ostiesibus bis dedit / idem aedem Volcani sua pecu/nia restituit / idem aedem Veneris sua pecu/nia constituit / idem aed(em) Fortunae sua pecu/nia constituit / idem aed(em) Cereris sua pecunia / constituit / idem pondera ad macellum / cum M(arco) Turriano sua pecu/nia fecit / idem aedem Spei sua pecunia constituit idem tribunal in foro mar/moreum fecit / huic statua inaurata d(ecurionum) d(ecreto) / p(ecunia) p(ublica) posita est / item ahenea d(ecurionum) d(ecreto) p(ecunia) p(ublica) posita / prox- ume tribunal quaes(toris) / propterea quod cum res publica / praedia sua venderet ob pol/[l]icitationem belli navalis / HS $\overline{XV}$CC rei publicae don- avit / hunc decuriones funere pu/blico effer(endum) censuerunt

For Publius Lucilius Gamala, son of Publius, grandson of Publius, great-grandson of Publius, aedile for the sacred things of Volkanus, aedile, co-opted as town councillor by decree of the town councillors without having had to pay the entrance fee, pontifex *(high priest of Volkanus), made* duovir *(mayor) in the assembly for five years with the power of* censor, *curator for raising and spending public money. When he had received from public means money for games, he gave it back and held them at his own expense.*

The same made out of his own money for paying the actors in theatrical games, a street with stones which is connected to the Forum from one gate to the other. The same gave a banquet to the citizens on 217 couches. The same gave twice out of his own money a lunch to the citizens of Ostia. The same restored the temple of Volcanus out of his own money. The same built a temple for Venus with his own money. The same built a temple for Fortuna with his own money. The same built a temple for Ceres with his own money. The same made weights at the meat market together with Marcus Turrianus with his own money. The same built a temple for Spes with his own money. The same made a marble tribunal *(speaker's platform) on the Forum. For him a gilded statue was placed by decree of the town councillors at public expense. In the same way by decree of the town councillors a statue of bronze was placed near the* tribunal *of the* quaestor *at public expense, for the following reason: when the city sold some of its properties because of a promise related to a sea battle, he donated 15,200* sestertii *to the city. The town councillors decreed to honour him with a public funeral.*

APPENDIX 4

THE INSCRIPTION IN HONOUR OF P. LUCILIUS GAMALA 'IUNIOR'

The inscription in honour of P. Lucilius Gamala 'iunior' (ca AD 117-180). *CIL* XIV 376; *AE* 1993, 417; Meiggs 1972, 558 no 2 (find place unknown; now in the Musei Vaticani, Galleria Lapidaria, inv. 6841; marble pilaster: 58.5 cm high; 20.2 cm long; 14.3 cm wide):

P(ublio) Lucilio P(ublii) f(ilio) / P(ublii) n(epoti) P(ublii) pronep(oti) Gamalae / aed(ili) sacr(is) Volcáni / eiusdem pr(aetori) tert(io) dec(urioni) / adléctó d(ecurionum) d(ecreto) infanti / IIvir(o) praéfectó L(ucii) Caesar(is) / Aug(usti) f(ilii) cens(ori) q(uaestori) a(erarii) pontif(ici) / tabulár(um) et librorum / curátori primo constitut(o) / hic ludós omnes quós fécit / amplificávit impensá sua / idem munus gladiatorium ded(it) / idem áedem Castoris et Pollucis rest(ituit) / idem curator pecuniae publicae exi/gendae et attribuenda in comi/tiis factus cellam patri Tiberino / restituit / idem thermas quas divus Pius aedifi/caverat vi ignis consumptas refecit / porticum reparavit / idem aedem Veneris impensa sua / restituit / idem pondera ad macellum et men/suras ad forum vinar(ium) s(ua) p(ecunia) fecit / idem navale a L(ucio) Coilio aedificatum / extru[e]ntibus(?) fere collapsum / restituit / huic statua aenea peq(unia) pub(lica) d(ecreto) d(ecurionum) posit(a) / est / [---]

For Publius Lucilius Gamala, son of Publius, grandson of Publius, great-grandson of Publius, aedile for the sacred things of Volcanus, praetor *of the same (god) for the third time, as child co-opted town councillor as child by decree of the town councillors,* duovir *(mayor), prefect of Lucius Caesar, son of the emperor,* censor, quaestor *of the town treasury,* pontifex *(high priest of Volcanus), first appointed* curator *of the records and the books. He expanded all games which he held at his own expense. The same gave a show of gladiators. The same restored the temple of Castor and Pollux. The same was made* curator *for raising and spending public money in the assembly. He restored the (temple-)cella for Father Tiberinus. The same restored the baths which the deified (Antoninus) Pius had built which had been destoyed by the force of fire. He restored the portico. The same restored the temple of Venus at his own expense. The same made weights for the meat market and measures for the Wine Forum with his own money. The same repaired the dockyard which had been built by Lucius Coilius and which had almost collapsed (when they were building it (?)). For him (Publius) a bronze statue is placed at public expense by decree of the town councillors [---].*

BIBLIOGRAPHY

AE: *L'Année Épigraphique* (supplement of *Revue Archéologique*), Paris 1888 -.

ALMAR, K.P., *Inscriptiones Latinae. Eine illustrierte Einführung in die lateinische Epigraphik*, Odense 1990.

BAKKER, J.TH., *Living and Working with the Gods. Studies of Evidence for Private Religion and its Material Environment in Ostia (100 BC-500 BC)*, Amsterdam 1994.

BARGAGLI, B./C. GROSSO, *I Fasti Ostienses*, Roma 1997.

BECATTI, G., *Case Ostiensi del tardo impero*, Roma 1949.

BECATTI, G. (ed.), *Scavi di Ostia* IV: *Mosaici e pavimenti marmorei*, Roma 1961.

BECK, R., *The Religion of the Mithras Cult in the Roman Empire. Mysteries of the Unconquered Sun*, Oxford 2006.

BLOCH, H., Ostia – Iscrizioni rinvenute tra il 1893 e il 1939, *NSc* 1953, 239-306.

BROUWER, H.H.J., *Bona Dea. De bronnen en een beschrijving van de cultus*, Utrecht 1982.

BOIN, D.R., Late Antique Ostia and a Campaign for Pious Tourism: Epitaphs for Bishop Cyriacus and Monica, Mother of Augustine, *Journal of Roman Studies* 100 (2010) 195-209.

BRENK, B./P. PENSABENE, Christliche Basilika oder christliche "Domus der Tigriniani"?, *Boreas* 21-22 (1998-1999) 271-299.

CARROLL, M., *Spirits of the Dead. Roman Funerary Commemoration in Western Europe*, Oxford 2006.

CÉBEILLAC-GERVASONI, M./M.L. CALDELLI/F. ZEVI, *Épigraphie latine*, Paris 2006 (*Epigrafia latina*, Roma 2010).

CIL: *Corpus Inscriptionum Latinarum*, Berolini/Berlin 1863 -:
Corpus Inscriptionum Latinarum XIV, Dessau, H. (ed.), Berolini/Berlin 1887.
Corpus Inscriptionum Latinarum XIV, *Supplementum*, Wickert, L. (ed.), Berolini/Berlin 1930.
Corpus Inscriptionum Latinarum XIV, *Fasciculus alter*, Wickert, L. (ed.), Berolini/Berlin 1933.

DESCŒUDRES, J.P. (ed.), *Ostia, port et porte de la Rome antique* (exp. cat. Genève), Genève 2001.
DUNBABIN, K.M.D., Inbide calco te… Trampling upon the Envious, in: *Tesserae. Festschrif für J. Engemann*, Münster 1991, 26-35.
GALLINA ZEVI, A./A. CLARIDGE (eds), *'Roman Ostia' Revisited. Archaeological and Historical Papers in Memory of Russell Meiggs*, Roma: Britisch School 1996.
GALLINA ZEVI, A./J.H. HUMPHREY (eds), *Ostia, Cicero, Gamala, Feasts, & The Economy. Papers in Memory of John H. D'Arms* (Journal of Roman Archaeology Suppl. Series 57). Portsmouth, Rhode Island 2004.
HEINZELMANN, M. (mit Beiträgen von A. Martin und C. Colini), *Die Nekropolen von Ostia. Untersuchungungen zu den Gräberstraßen vor der Porta Romana und an der Via Laurentina*, München 2000.
HELBIG, W., *Führer durch die öffentlichen Sammlungen klassischer Altertümer in Rom* IV, Tübingen 1972 (fourth edition).
HERES, T.L., Paries. *A Proposal for a Dating System of Late-Antique Masonry Structures in Rome and Ostia AD 235-600*, Amsterdam 1982.
HERMANSEN, G., *Ostia: aspects of Roman city life*, Edmonton 1981.
Hermeneus 70, 2 (1998): Dutch journal, thematical fascicle on Ostia.
HERZ, P., Claudius Abascantus aus Ostia. Die Nomenklatur eines libertus und sein sozialer Aufstieg, *Zeitschrift für Papyrologie und Epigraphik* 76, 1989, 167-174.
HÜTTEMAN, A., *Pompejanische Inschriften. Der heutige Bestand vor Ort im Stadtgebiet und in der Nekropolen*, Stuttgart: Philipp Reclam 2010.
JONES, C.P., The pancratiasts Helix and Alexander on an Ostian mosaic, *Journal of Roman Archaeology* 11, 1998, 293-298.
MEIGGS, R., *Roman Ostia*, Oxford 1973 (second edition).
MOLS, S.T.A.M., Filosofen te kakken gezet? Geschilderde filosofenportretten in Ostia, *Lampas* 30 (1997) 360-371.
MOLS, S.T.A.M./C.E. VAN DER LAAN (eds), *Papers of the Netherlands Institute in Rome, Antiquity* 58, 1999 (thematical fascicle on Ostia).
NICOLET, C. (ed.), Ports et avants-ports: la ville et la mer, *Mélanges de l'École française de Rome. Antiquité* 114, 2002, 1-449.
NOTERMANS, A., *Spekende mozaïeken. Functie en betekenis van teksten op Romeinse vloermozaïeken*, Nijmegen (PhD dissertation Radboud University) 1997.
NSc: *Notizie degli Scavi di Antichità*.
PAVOLINI, C., *Ostia*, Roma/Bari 2006 (revised edition).
PAVOLINI, C., *La vita quotidiana a Ostia*, Roma 1986.
PENSABENE, P., *Ostiensium marmorium decus et decor. Studi architettonici,*

decorativi e archeometrici (Studi Miscellanei 33), Roma 2007.
RIEGER, A.-K., *Heiligtümer in Ostia*, München 2004.
SEG: *Supplementum Epigraphicum Graecum* (also online). Leiden 1923 -.
STEUERNAGEL, D., *Kult und Alltag in römischen Hafenstädten. Soziale Prozesse in archäologischer Perspektive*, Wiesbaden 2004.
STRASSER, J.-Y., Les Antôninia Pythia de Rome, *Nikephoros* 17, 2004, 201-207.
VAN DER MEER, L.B., with N.L.C. Stevens, and Stöger, H., Domus Fulminata, *BABesch* 80 (2005) 91-111.
VAN DER MEER, L.B., The Temple on the Piazzale delle Corporazioni in Ostia Antica, *BABESCH* 84 (2009) 163-170.
VARONE, A., *Erotica Pompeiana. Love Inscriptions on the Walls of Pompeii*, Roma 2002.
ZEVI, F., Il tempio del collegio dei fabri tignuarii e una dedica a Pertinace divinizzato (Miscellanea Ostiense III), *Rendiconti dell'Accademia dei Lincei* 26 (1971) 472-478.

Websites:
Ostia – Harbour of Ancient Rome (webmaster: Jan Theo Bakker):
http://www.ostia-antica.org/

Epigraphische Datenbank Heidelberg (EDH):
http://www.uni-heidelberg.de/institute/sonst/adw/edh/

INDEX

ager publicus
  5, 7, 13, 45, 48-49
Alexandria
  26, 28, 31, 36, 76, 94
annona
  6, 10, 29, 31, 41-42, 45, 55, 60-61, 116
Antoninus Pius
  22, 28, 57, 58-59, 61, 117, 121
apotropaic elements
  91-92, 104
aqueduct
  9, 15
Augustine
  60, 88-90, 92, 123
Augustus
  5, 8, 10, 11, 13, 20, 25, 27, 29, 41, 52-54, 65, 67, 79, 82, 112, 115, 117
bakery
  21
bar
  7, 19, 20, 26-27, 75, 79, 84
barracks
  2, 19-22, 25-27
baths
  7-9, 15-18, 33, 53, 55, 58-62, 68-69, 72, 74-75, 78, 85-86, 91, 93, 98, 104, 121
benefaction
  41, 84
Bona Dea
  14, 82-84

brothel
  75
building techniques
  7-8
Caligula
  15, 117
Caracalla
  9, 22, 25, 117
castrum
  4-5, 15, 90
Ceres
  38, 40, 45, 71, 120
Christian religion
  8-9, 29-30, 52, 69, 71, 77, 87-88, 92, 94-96, 99, 107
Cicero
  5, 7, 14, 16, 82, 84, 98, 110
Claudius
  1, 6, 11, 14-15, 20, 31, 38, 51, 117
Claudius Pulcher
  14
Commodus
  7, 22, 28, 31, 47, 58, 117
Constantine
  6, 8, 118
Cybele
  7, 37, 98-99
damnatio memoriae
  2, 22, 47, 69
decumanus
  5, 9, 13, 15, 19, 28-29, 47-50, 53, 84, 87-88, 90, 92, 107

decurio
  10, 37, 40-41, 44-45, 58, 49, 61, 80, 109-110, 115, 119
Diocletian
  66, 118
Dionysus
  63, 99
Dioscuri
  50, 104
Domitian
  6, 20, 38, 85, 117
domus
  8-9, 30, 50, 79, 88-89, 92-94, 98
duumvir (*duovir*)
  7, 9, 41, 46, 67, 80, 81-82, 109, 119, 121
emperor cult
  6-8, 10, 21, 25, 31, 38, 41
erasion
  2, 22-23, 25, 31, 40, 66
euergetism (see benefaction)
Fasti Ostienses
  5, 20, 56, 76, 123
firemen
  2, 8, 19-27, 116
fish
  16, 33, 64, 75, 90-92, 94-97, 103
Fortuna
  26, 45, 62, 65, 96, 102, 119
forum
  4-5, 8, 10, 21, 32, 37, 41-42, 47, 53-57, 60, 65, 92, 102, 110-111, 121-122
fountain (see *nymphaeum*)
freedman (see *libertus*)
funeral
  20, 41, 110, 112, 120
Gamala
  45-46, 51, 80, 84, 119-122
games
  18, 41, 50, 51, 85, 111, 119-121
gate
  5, 9, 11, 14, 16, 19, 21, 27, 29, 78, 84, 112, 120
Gordian
  21-22, 118
grain
  5-10, 28-29, 31, 34-45, 49, 51, 54-55, 61, 66, 70, 78, 107-108, 116
granary
  6, 20, 28, 48, 70, 107
guild
  6, 18, 31-33, 36, 38-41, 44, 47, 56, 60-62, 69, 70, 87-88, 91, 98, 101-102, 110, 114, 116
Hadrian
  6-7, 16, 20, 22-23, 28, 37-38, 40-41, 44, 47, 52-53, 56, 72, 74, 76, 78, 85, 109-110, 117
Heliogabalus
  85, 117
Hercules
  5, 39, 52-53, 63-67, 112
horrea
  28, 48, 62, 70, 78, 102, 107
insula
  2, 6
jealousy
  90-91, 103
Jews
  7, 45
Julia Domna
  22, 25
Jupiter
  7, 46, 50, 53, 76, 104
libertus
  6-8, 10, 31, 42, 46, 62, 69, 76, 99-101, 108-111, 115

ligature
  49, 101
Magna mater (see Cybele)
Marcus Aurelius
  22-23, 25, 28, 37, 117
marriage
  14, 44, 61-62
Mars
  10, 42, 44, 104
mayor, see *duumvir*
memory
  2, 22, 47, 63, 69
Mithras
  7, 33, 65, 68, 78, 97, 104-107
money
  11, 29, 38, 100, 111, 115, 119-122
mosaic
  1, 8, 16, 19, 21, 26-27, 31-37, 45-46, 50, 62, 70-72, 74-79, 84-86, 88, 90, 92, 94, 103-108, 112
neighbourhood
  52, 78, 83
Neptunus
  10, 16, 50, 68, 86, 96
Nero
  6, 11, 13, 20
North Africa
  5, 13, 28, 31-36, 39, 41
nymphaeum
  8-9, 47, 83, 88-89, 92
overwriting
  67
painting
  1, 23, 51, 53, 62, 68-69, 72, 73, 75, 94
Pertinax
  23, 28, 47, 58, 99, 117, 125
planets
  104-106

Pompeii
  18, 26, 75, 102, 124
Poplicola
  46, 67, 80-82
Portus (*uterque*)
  1, 6, 8-9, 21, 29, 33, 45, 50-51, 79, 87, 119
Pozzuoli (Puteoli)
  6, 20, 85
public horse
  37, 77
restoration
  8-9, 14, 28-29, 45, 51, 54-55, 59, 60, 83, 89, 120-121
reuse (see *spolia*)
Roma
  5, 10, 30, 40, 53-54, 111
Rome
  4-6, 8-11, 13-15, 18, 20, 27-29, 42, 45-46, 48-52, 54-55, 61, 65, 70, 76-77, 83, 84-89, 92, 98-99, 101, 105, 111, 114
salt
  4
Sardinia
  5, 31, 35, 39
self-representation
  83
Septimius Severus
  7, 22, 25, 28, 41, 47, 56, 87, 100, 117
Serapis
  7, 69, 76, 77, 108
sex
  53, 75, 85
shipmasters
  32-36
shop
  7, 13, 16, 29, 62, 78, 79, 84, 90-92, 98, 103

Silvanus
    44-45
slave
    6, 29, 31, 98, 101, 109
Sol (Sun)
    104-108
Spes
    45, 119-120
spolia
    8, 42
sponsoring
    31, 41, 45
sport (see games)
storehouse (see *horrea*)
statio (office)
    36, 40-41, 74, 91
superscript
    25
synagogue
    7, 10, 98
temple
    5-8, 10, 21, 26, 31-33, 38-42, 45,
    47, 51, 53, 60, 63, 67, 70-71, 76,
    82, 87, 98, 102, 107, 110, 120-121
theatre
    5, 7, 9-10, 13, 27-42
Theodosius
    51, 118
Tiberius
    11, 15, 20, 51, 117
Titus
    40, 117
town council(lors) (see *decurio*)
transport
    4, 16, 35-36, 98
Trajan
    1, 6, 23, 28, 57, 62, 72, 88, 117
Venus
    6, 10, 42, 44-45, 62, 72, 86, 91,
    104, 120-121

Vespasian
    15, 40
vicus
    21, 52
Vulcanus
    8, 10, 37-38, 45, 80, 100-101,
    119
workshop
    7, 32-33, 62, 87